M000273693

# SYMBOLS
# IN
# GRAPHIC
# DESIGN

SendPoints

# SYMBOLS
# IN GRAPHIC DESIGN

© 2016 SendPoints Publishing Co., Ltd.

**SendPoints**

**EDITED & PUBLISHED BY** SendPoints Publishing Co., Ltd.

**PUBLISHER:** Lin Gengli

**PUBLISHING DIRECTOR:** Lin Shijian

**CHIEF EDITOR:** Lin Shijian

**EXECUTIVE EDITOR:** Li Weiji

**ART DIRECTOR:** He Wanling

**EXECUTIVE ART EDITOR:** Look Hoi Yan

**PROOFREADING:** Luo Yanmei

**REGISTERED ADDRESS:** Room 15A Block 9 Tsui Chuk Garden, Wong Tai Sin, Kowloon, Hong Kong

**TEL:** +852-35832323 / **FAX:** +852-35832448

**OFFICE ADDRESS:** 7F, 9th Anning Street, Jinshazhou, Baiyun District, Guangzhou, China

**TEL:** +86-20-89095121 / **FAX:** +86-20-89095206

**BEIJING OFFICE:** Room 107, Floor 1, Xiyingfang Alley, Ande Road, Dongcheng District, Beijing, China

**TEL:** +86-10-84139071 / **FAX:** +86-10-84139071

**SHANGHAI OFFICE:** Room 307, Building 1, Hong Qiang Creative, Zhabei District, Shanghai, China

**TEL:** +86-21-63523469 / **FAX:** +86-21-63523469

**SALES MANAGER:** Sissi

**TEL:** +86-20-81007895

**EMAIL:** overseas01@sendpoints.cn

**WEBSITE:** www.sendpoints.cn / www.spbooks.cn

**ISBN** 978-988-77572-5-2

All rights reserved. No part of this publication may be reproduced, stored in a retrieval system or transmitted in any form or by any means, electronic, mechanical, photocopying, recording or otherwise, without prior permission in writing from the publisher. For more information, please contact SendPoints Publishing Co., Ltd.

Printed and bound in China.

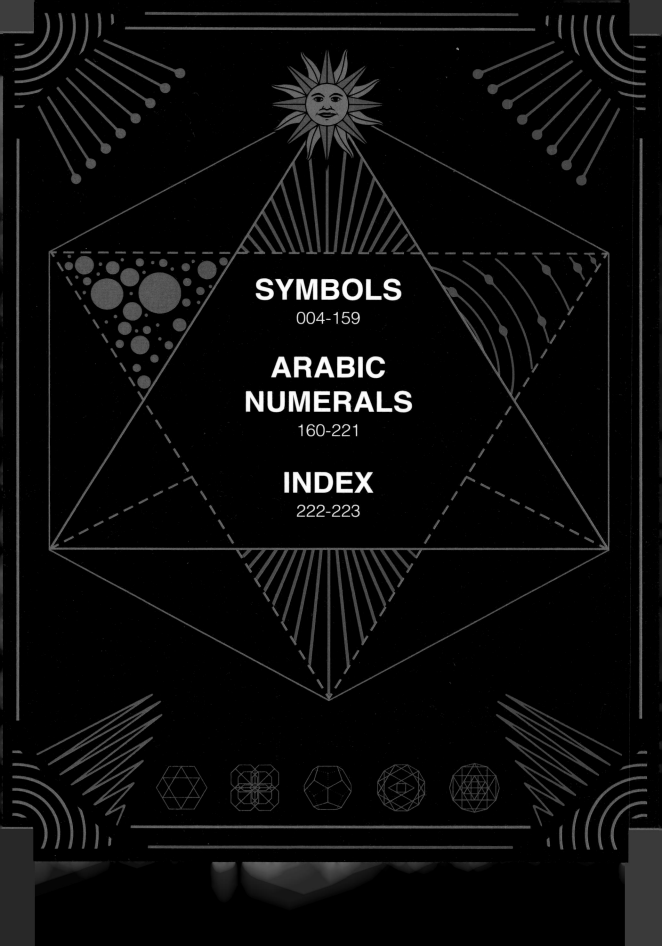

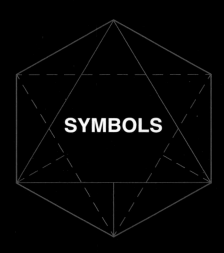

SYMBOLS

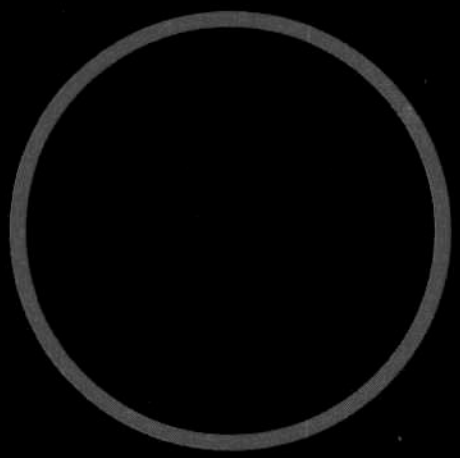

Circle   Wholeness   Infinity

Square   Structure   Masculinity

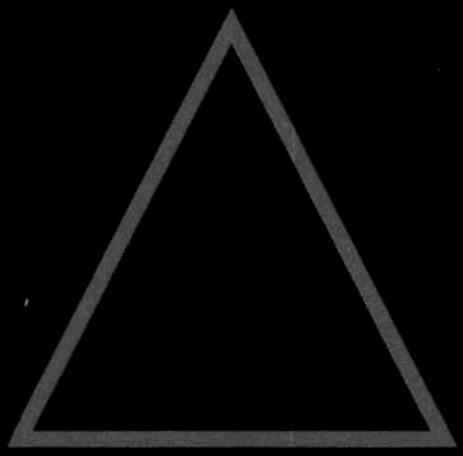

Triangle   Balance   Wisdom

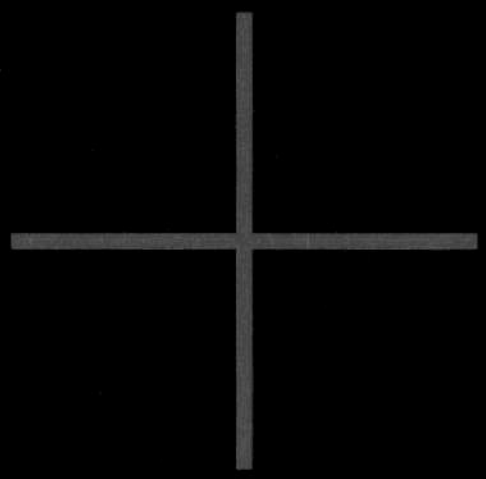

Cross   Orientation   Sacredness

Nuclear disarmament   Flag Semaphore   Peace

Philosopher's Stone   Alchemy   Immortality

Triskele   Celts   Energy

Ankh   Egyptian Glyph   Life

Inti   Incan Sun God   Heraldry

Crossed Arrows   North American Indians   Friendship

Veve of Maman   Brigitte Voodoo   Loa of Death

The Rod of Asclepius   Greek Mythology   Healing

Symbols, or let's say the graphic symbols that we focus on in this book, are a primal form of human communication, representing concrete objects, numbers, social status, and eventually abstract ideas or emotions. They appeared spontaneously in various civilizations across the world.

# Historical Traces

The cuneiform, an ancient written language developed by Sumerians of Mesopotamia in about 3500 B.C., had a pictographic form in its earliest phase which originated in the need of making agricultural and trading records. In other words, these pictographs were symbols. The symbols were primarily impressed on hollow clay containers to show the type and quantity of the clay tokens inside, long before they were inscribed on the wet clay tablets with a reed stylus leading to the later wedge-shaped cuneiform.

In China, ancient symbols were found on animal bones, turtle plastrons, pottery, and the cliff carvings in Neolithic sites. In spite of their fragmentary expression, these symbols are often compared with the oracle bone script in Shang Dynasty, which is considered the first Chinese written language developed in around 1200 B.C. Although the identification of these symbols still remains controversial, they disclose the common usage of signs and symbols in communication regardless of time and space.

Symbols are also a common communication tool for North American Indians. Deciphering these symbols is the key to understanding their mysterious culture. For instance, the highly identifiable symbols include two arrows pointing in opposite directions for war, a broken arrow for peace, and crossed arrows for friendship. The often found face paint is crucial in ceremonies and frightens enemy in war, for example. the handprint symbol painted on their faces, body and their horses was believed to endow the bearers with energy.

In the civilized societies, graphic symbols evolved into a compressed signifier consisting of multiple meanings, and then naturally developed into more complex shapes and forms. Heraldry is an exemplar of graphic symbols' refinement in structure and connotation. Both Europe and Japan enjoy a long history of heraldry, which began as an identifiable sign for warriors in battle and later became an emblem for clans or individuals. Heraldry in Europe is highly ornate, normally featuring animals, shield, motto and other embellishments, with different colors and elements conveying different messages. On the contrary, Japanese heraldry, named mon or kamon, prefers a natural context and uses mainly botanical symbols in a simple structure and color scheme.

# Legends, Religions and Occult

Human being lives upon nature, and there has been a deeply ingrained belief in the existence of supernatural power even in modern era. The unknown powers were always represented by graphic symbols and even particular characters in mystical stories. One can easily notice that some films and televisions with the theme of magic or superheroes would adopt or recreate some symbols to complement the mysterious setting.

The widely employed symbol of a serpent twining around a rod in logos especially of hospital or medical organization is the Rod of Asclepius. Asclepius is a god of healing and medicine in Greek mythology who always carries with him this magical rod. It's worth mentioning that a rod with double wings and serpents, namely the caduceus, is sometimes mistakenly used instead of the rod of Asclepius.

As an icon of Christianity, the cross symbolizes the crucifixion and salvation of Jesus Christ, but in early time the believers were reluctant to use the cross symbol because of the pain it suggested. The hexagram Star of David has not been widely used as the symbol of Judaism until the 19 century. It was adopted allegedly from the Seal of Solomon, yet this hexagram was found in other cultures as well. In the religious rituals of Haitian Voodoo, a veve symbol is usually drawn in an attempt to communicate and send wishes to the spirits, Loa.

The Freemasonry, a long-established underground fraternity organization, has its emblem featured with the square and compasses for its founding background, and uses a lot of symbols due to the illiteracy of masons at that time. Alchemists in the ancient times had to acquire the use of a series of esoteric symbols. The symbols are mostly geometric forms such as the triangular symbols of four elements, and animals such as the ouroboros where a serpent is holding its tail in the mouth.

# Modern Graphic Symbols

These graphic symbols of hundreds or thousands of years old have attained a refined structure and form, and are the essence of human wisdom and civilization. They have been given different connotations with the passage of time; this explains why they are exuberant and long-lasting. Nowadays, we are surrounded by different types of graphic symbols: the antique star signs, mathematical and music notations, and the contemporary way-finding icons, digital interface icons, and brand logo, etc. In 1958, Gerald Holtom designed a logo for the Campaign for Nuclear Disarmament, taking the N and D signals from flag semaphore as the basis, and now it has become a world recognized symbol of peace. In the 1970s, Milton Glaser created the I♥NY rebus as the logo for New York City but it has gone viral throughout the world. Its significance grows as the city goes through sorrow and happiness.

People look at different lines and shapes with particular emotional experience, which the graphic designers take into account when they try to manipulate his or her design materials. In modern graphic design, as design thinking develops, other than the prominent logos and the highly functional icons, supplementary graphic symbols are gaining special attention from designers. They are normally in an abstract form or shape, embedded with designers' ingenuity and imagination, affecting viewer's perception of the subject matter. Some of them are accessible in an inspiring way, while some require interpretation to understand the connotation and the mechanism behind their appeal.

We believe that graphic designers are creators of modern-day graphic symbols.

**Projects**
*014*
*/*
*159*

# Yuki Ota Fencing Championship

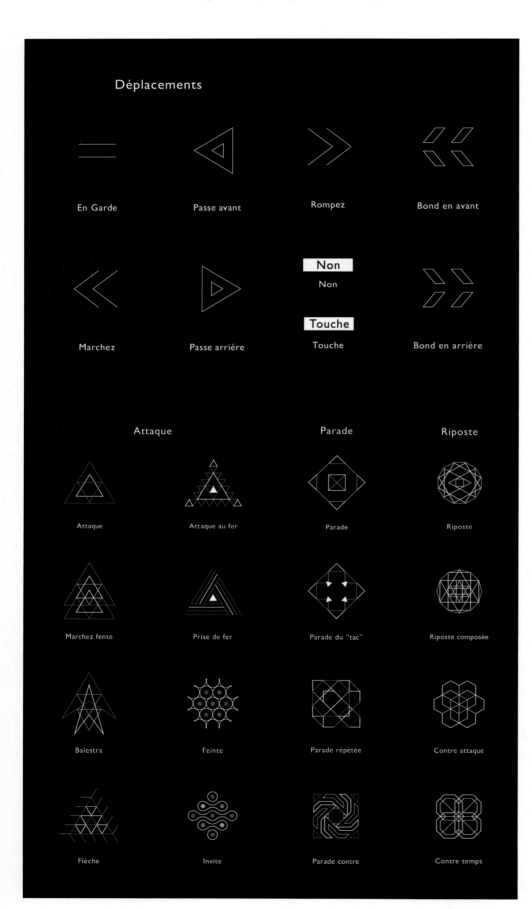

Based on the theme of the championship—"Visualized Fencing", the sophisticated movements and complicated techniques of a fight, such as the attack and parry, have been interpreted as different symbols in the visual communication. By visualizing the trajectory of the movements and techniques of manipulating a sword, the designers aimed to make fencing easier to understand by more people.

**Creative Director: Kaoru Sugano**
**Art Director: Yuri Uenishi**
**Designer: Yuri Uenishi, Toshinori Obuchi, Megumi Gotanda**

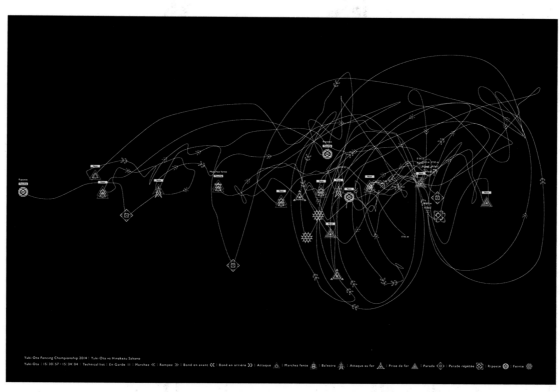

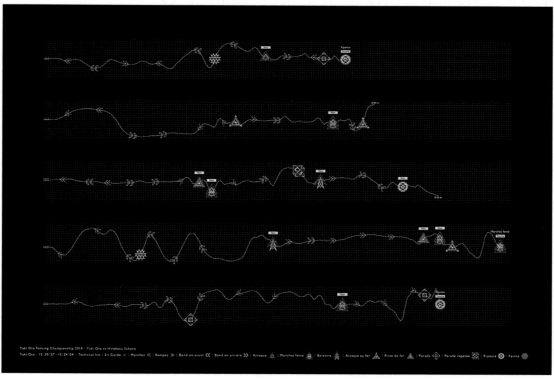

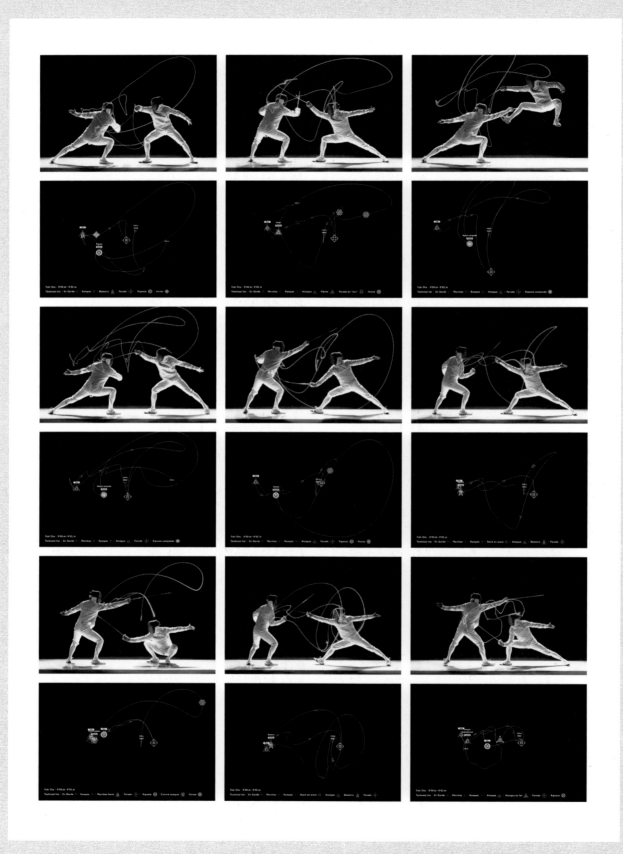

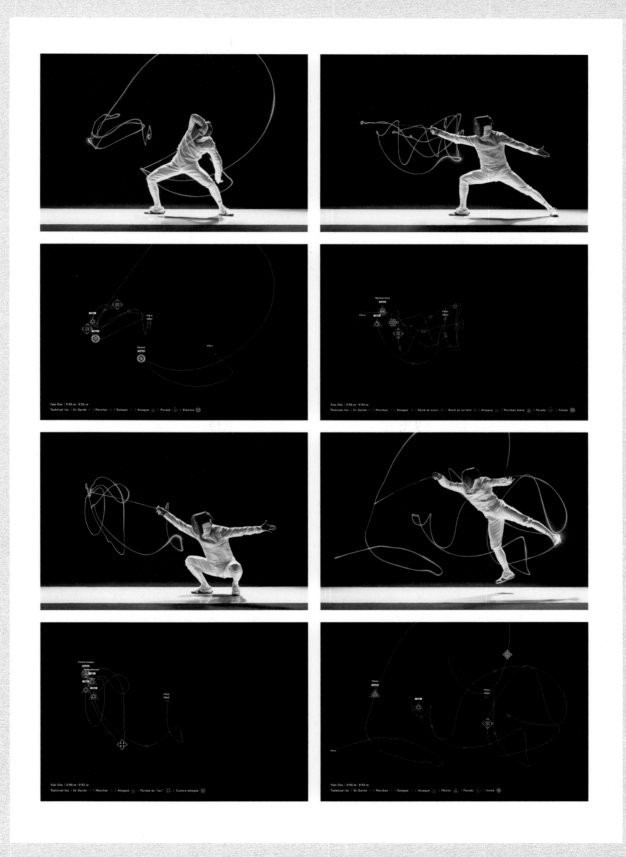

# Binary Finger System Calendar

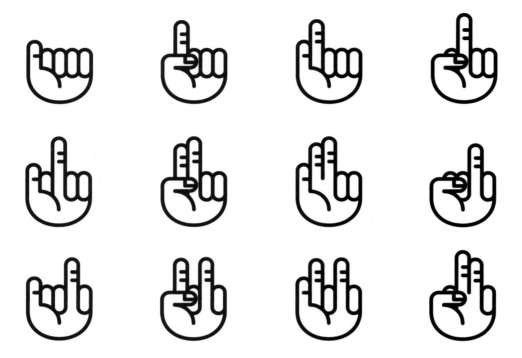

Finger binary is a system for counting and displaying numbers on the fingers of one or more hands. The calendar is a graphic visualization of the twelve months in this seldom used counting system.

**Designer: Albert Wijaya**

| s | m | t | w | t | f | s |
|---|---|---|---|---|---|---|
| | | | 1 | 2 | 3 | 4 |
| **5** | 6 | 7 | 8 | 9 | 10 | 11 |
| **12** | 13 | 14 | 15 | 16 | 17 | 18 |
| **19** | 20 | 21 | 22 | 23 | 24 | 25 |
| **26** | 27 | 28 | 29 | 30 | 31 | |

| s | m | t | w | t | f | s |
|---|---|---|---|---|---|---|
| | | | | | | 1 |
| **2** | 3 | 4 | 5 | 6 | 7 | 8 |
| **9** | 10 | 11 | 12 | 13 | 14 | 15 |
| **16** | 17 | 18 | 19 | 20 | 21 | 22 |
| **23** | 24 | 25 | 26 | 27 | 28 | |

| s | m | t | w | t | f | s |
|---|---|---|---|---|---|---|
| | | | | | | 1 |
| **2** | 3 | 4 | 5 | 6 | 7 | 8 |
| **9** | 10 | 11 | 12 | 13 | 14 | 15 |
| **16** | 17 | 18 | 19 | 20 | 21 | 22 |
| **23** | 24 | 25 | 26 | 27 | 28 | 29 |
| **30** | 31 | | | | | |

| s | m | t | w | t | f | s |
|---|---|---|---|---|---|---|
| | | 1 | 2 | 3 | 4 | 5 |
| **6** | 7 | 8 | 9 | 10 | 11 | 12 |
| **13** | 14 | 15 | 16 | 17 | 18 | 19 |
| **20** | 21 | 22 | 23 | 24 | 25 | 26 |
| **27** | 28 | 29 | 30 | | | |

| s | m | t | w | t | f | s |
|---|---|---|---|---|---|---|
| | | | | 1 | 2 | 3 |
| **4** | 5 | 6 | 7 | 8 | 9 | 10 |
| **11** | 12 | 13 | 14 | 15 | 16 | 17 |
| **18** | 19 | 20 | 21 | 22 | 23 | 24 |
| **25** | 26 | 27 | 28 | 29 | 30 | 31 |

| s | m | t | w | t | f | s |
|---|---|---|---|---|---|---|
| **1** | 2 | 3 | 4 | 5 | 6 | 7 |
| **8** | 9 | 10 | 11 | 12 | 13 | 14 |
| **15** | 16 | 17 | 18 | 19 | 20 | 21 |
| **22** | 23 | 24 | 25 | 26 | 27 | 28 |
| **29** | 30 | | | | | |

| s | m | t | w | t | f | s |
|---|---|---|---|---|---|---|
| | | 1 | 2 | 3 | 4 | 5 |
| **6** | 7 | 8 | 9 | 10 | 11 | 12 |
| **13** | 14 | 15 | 16 | 17 | 18 | 19 |
| **20** | 21 | 22 | 23 | 24 | 25 | 26 |
| **27** | 28 | 29 | 30 | 31 | | |

| s | m | t | w | t | f | s |
|---|---|---|---|---|---|---|
| | | | | | 1 | 2 |
| **3** | 4 | 5 | 6 | 7 | 8 | 9 |
| **10** | 11 | 12 | 13 | 14 | 15 | 16 |
| **17** | 18 | 19 | 20 | 21 | 22 | 23 |
| **24** | 25 | 26 | 27 | 28 | 29 | 30 |
| **31** | | | | | | |

| s | m | t | w | t | f | s |
|---|---|---|---|---|---|---|
| | 1 | 2 | 3 | 4 | 5 | 6 |
| **7** | 8 | 9 | 10 | 11 | 12 | 13 |
| **14** | 15 | 16 | 17 | 18 | 19 | 20 |
| **21** | 22 | 23 | 24 | 25 | 26 | 27 |
| **28** | 29 | 30 | | | | |

| s | m | t | w | t | f | s |
|---|---|---|---|---|---|---|
| | | | 1 | 2 | 3 | 4 |
| **5** | 6 | 7 | 8 | 9 | 10 | 11 |
| **12** | 13 | 14 | 15 | 16 | 17 | 18 |
| **19** | 20 | 21 | 22 | 23 | 24 | 25 |
| **26** | 27 | 28 | 29 | 30 | 31 | |

| s | m | t | w | t | f | s |
|---|---|---|---|---|---|---|
| | | | | | | 1 |
| **2** | 3 | 4 | 5 | 6 | 7 | 8 |
| **9** | 10 | 11 | 12 | 13 | 14 | 15 |
| **16** | 17 | 18 | 19 | 20 | 21 | 22 |
| **23** | 24 | 25 | 26 | 27 | 28 | 29 |
| **30** | | | | | | |

| s | m | t | w | t | f | s |
|---|---|---|---|---|---|---|
| | 1 | 2 | 3 | 4 | 5 | 6 |
| **7** | 8 | 9 | 10 | 11 | 12 | 13 |
| **14** | 15 | 16 | 17 | 18 | 19 | 20 |
| **21** | 22 | 23 | 24 | 25 | 26 | 27 |
| **28** | 29 | 30 | 31 | | | |

# Keukenconfessies

For the visual identity of the food design studio Keukenconfessies, the design team searched for a mixture of moods, colors, prints and printing techniques and came up with different, independent symbolic shapes inspired by food and cooking. The simplicity of these symbols allows for endless combinations and delivers a dynamic brand image. The black and bold lettertype gives a robust feeling next to the colorful shapes.

**Studio: Raw Color**

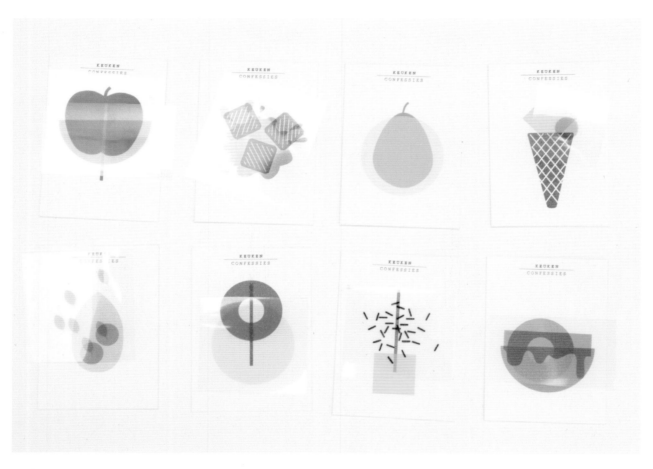

# Gifted & Talented Education

# Gifted and Talented Education

Gifted & Talented Education is a center set up by a group of specialists, nurturing high ability learners aged between 5 and 12 with differentiated education models. Inspired by the history of gifted education, the logo features the first institution of higher education—the symbolic Academy of Athens, while the three illustration symbols featured with famous historical figures represent different programs.

**Designer: Barbara Ng**

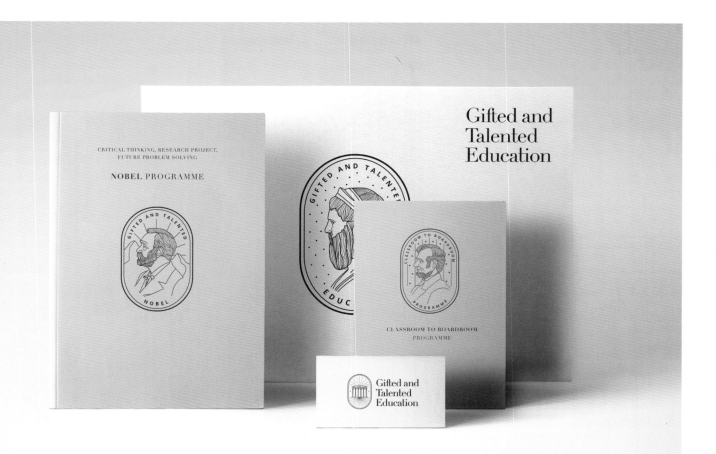

# (R)Evolution, Atlas of Innovation

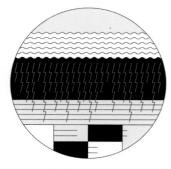

CHAPTER I — Italy
Place of innovation: Marina di Pisa, Italy.
Transforming the force of the sea waves into electricity.

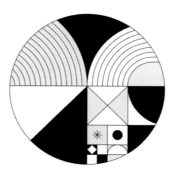

CHAPTER II—Europe
Place of innovation: Paris, France.
Facebook gathers and categorizes big amount of data with the aim of predicting the user's needs.

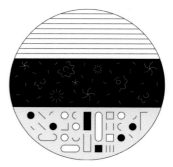

CHAPTER III—America
Place of innovation: Key Largo, Florida.
A laboratory anchored underwater used for training astronauts.

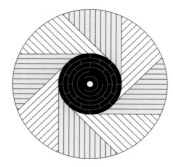

CHAPTER IV—Africa
Place of innovation: Port Louis, Mauritius.
The first woman president of the Mauritus is also a biodiversity scientist that is changing the nature of his country.

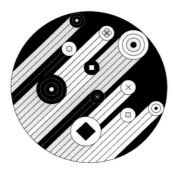

CHAPTER V—Asia
Place of innovation: Guangzhou, China.
The rising of the new Chinese enterprises.

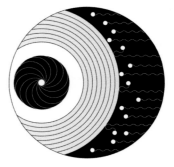

CHAPTER VI—Oceania
Place of innovation: Wollongong, Australia.
"Geldom", a new condom made from water.

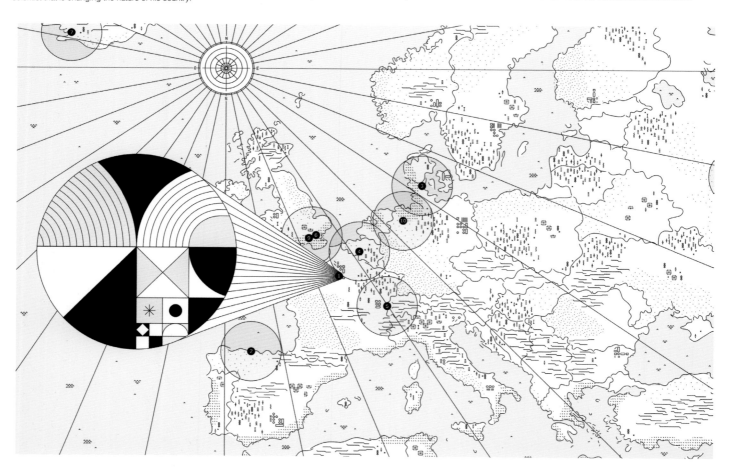

This is a collection of maps, illustrations and chapter openers for the magazine *Wired Italia*'s 76th issue: (R)Evolution, The Atlas of Innovation. In the maps, the mountains, beaches and cities are represented by various geometric symbols related to technology and information field, while every first place of innovation in the chapter is emphasized by a magnified circular symbol connected to the report on the place.

**Studio: La Tigre**
**Art Director: David Moretti, Massimo Pitis**

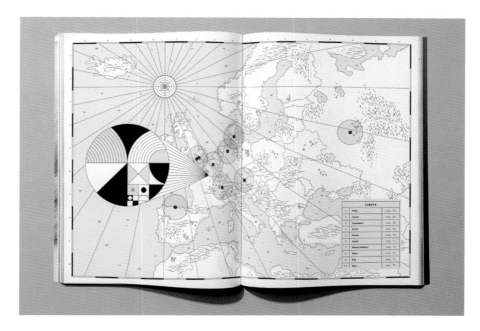

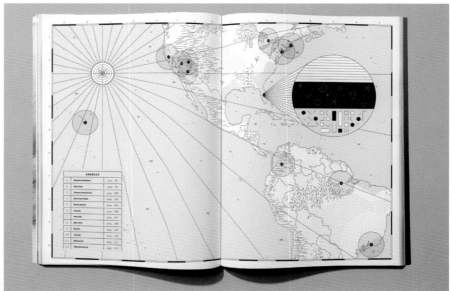

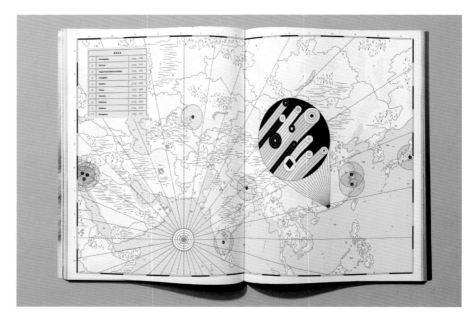

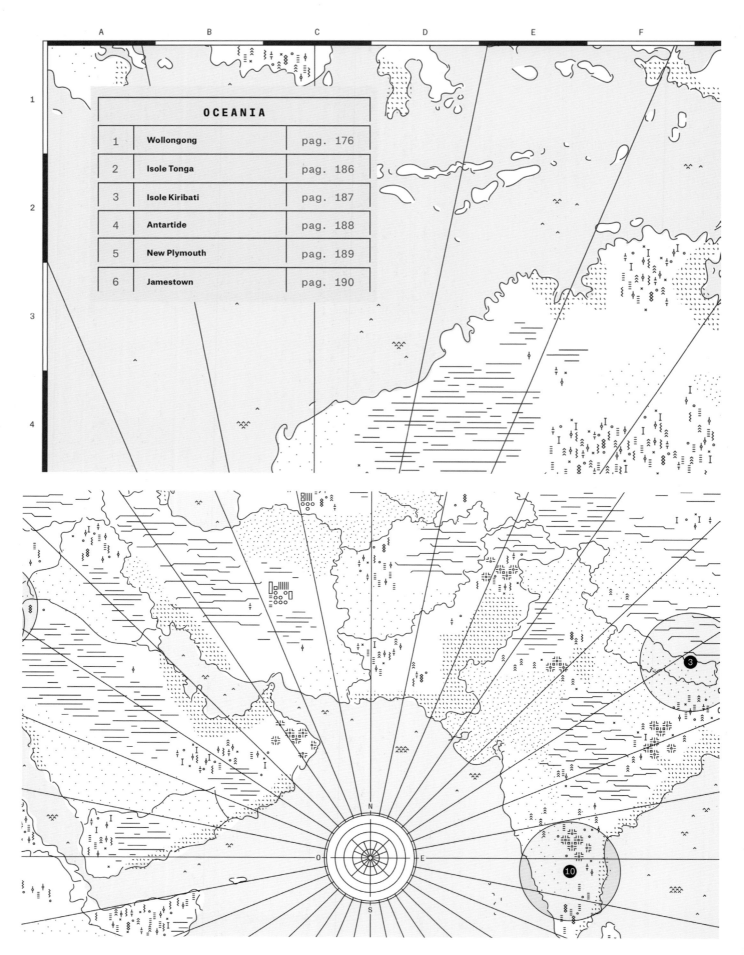

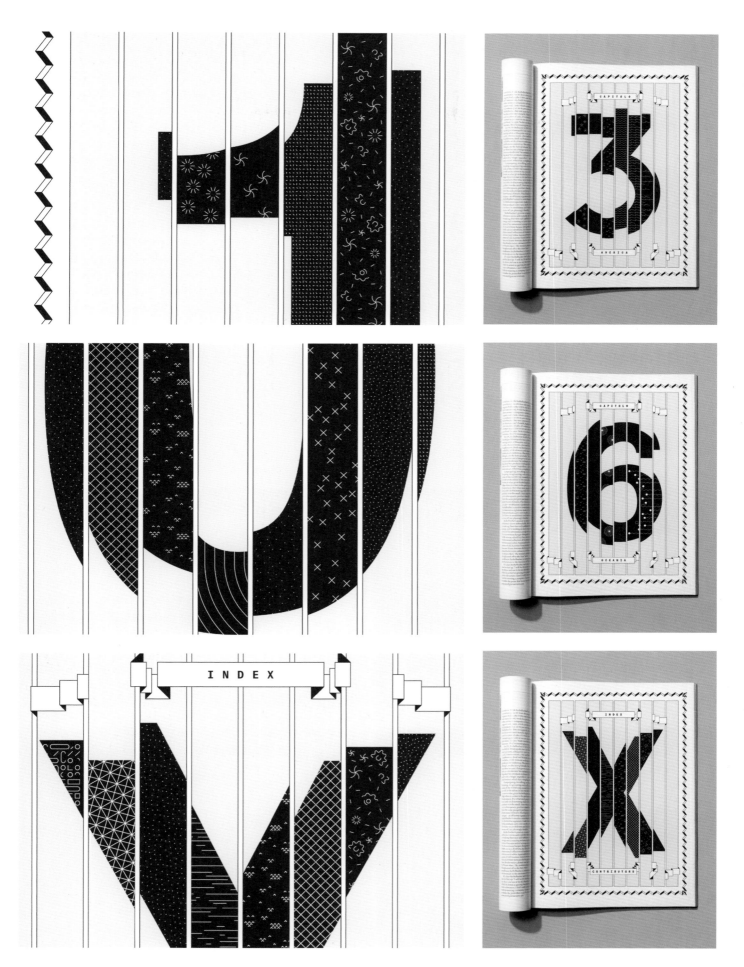

# OFFF Unmasked

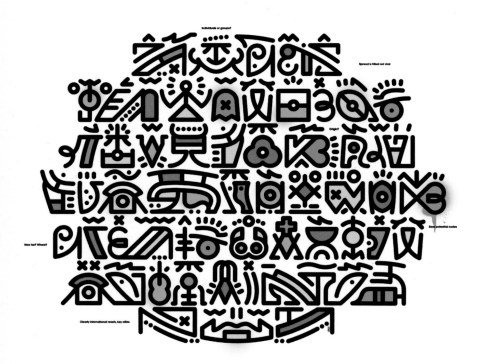

As an international festival for the post digital creation culture, OFFF invited renowned illustrators and graphic designers to design its art book—*OFFF Unmasked*. Marta Cerdà did the "scriptures" part for the book. The symbols illustration she designed is an imaginary alphabet that presents the theme in its most unique way.

**Designer: Marta Cerdà**

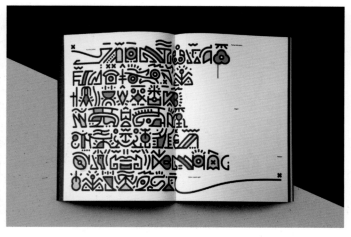

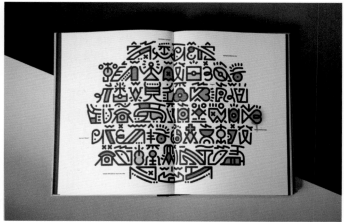

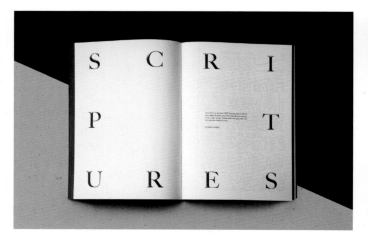

Founding father?

Past yet still present

Origin?

Genitor?

Hidden in plain sight

Gathering, sea, waves.

Vibrations?

Antoni G + OFFF = digital basilicas?

Mediterranean: owners of the image

# You Are the April of This World

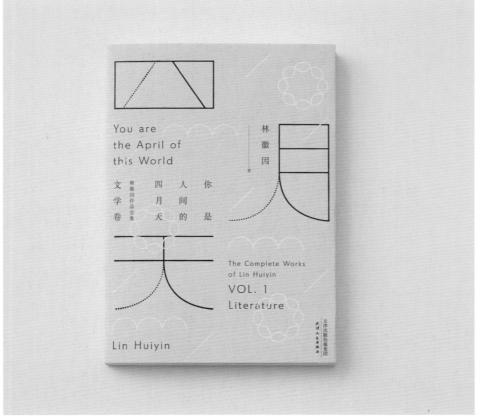

This complete work collection consists of two volumes: literature and architecture. The title is the name of a poem included in the collection. Based on this particular poem, the book designer chose six keywords for the graphic development—cloud, star, rain, flower, snow and water—and transformed them into graphic symbols. It is a kind of rational analysis of sensitivity and poetic imagery.

**Designer: Wang Zhi-Hong**

# Something Happening Somewhere

The album cover is based upon the Rendlesham Forest incident, a significant UFO incident with many reported sightings of unusual lights and landing craft in Suffolk, England in 1980. The whimsical symbols are a refined version of the glyphs found and drawn by a policeman when he examined the craft.

**Studio: Mainstudio**

# Wu Yang Xin Mi

天養

TIANYANG

所谓天养,相其时也,
只选取最适合水稻生长的时节育种,使其播种、生长、成熟、收
割都顺应了季节的变化,达到最佳的生长状态。

地養

DIYANG

所谓地养,择其处也,
武义山川秀美,自然环境得天独厚,境内丘陵蜿蜒起伏,形成
宜平武义两大盆地,造就了水稻生长的绝佳环境。

人養

RENYANG

所谓人养,精其业也,
汲取世代积累的农作经验,从选种到培育直至收割的每一个环
节都是人工悉心照料,如同艺术品一般精雕细琢。

水養

SHUIYANG

所谓水养,净其源也,
武义同为钱塘江水系和瓯江水系的源头,拥有浙江最清澈的山
泉水,以山泉水滋养的大米味甘性平,温润可口。

氣養

QIYANG

所谓气养,合其候也,
中亚热带季风气候造就了水稻绝佳的生长气候,而高达72%
的森林覆盖率,让水稻在洁净的空气中自由呼吸。

This is a packaging design for the organic rice produced by an ecological agricultural brand. The designer has devised five simple but quintessential symbols to visualize the product's five concepts of health preserving—celestial, earth, human, water and qi (life energy). The plain color is a reminder of the nature and purity of organic rice.

**Designer: Tang Shipeng**

# Noodle Theater

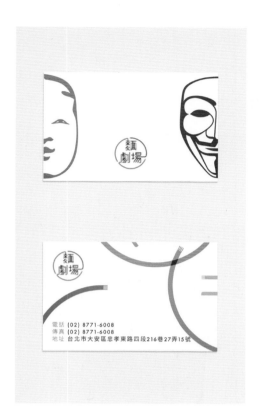

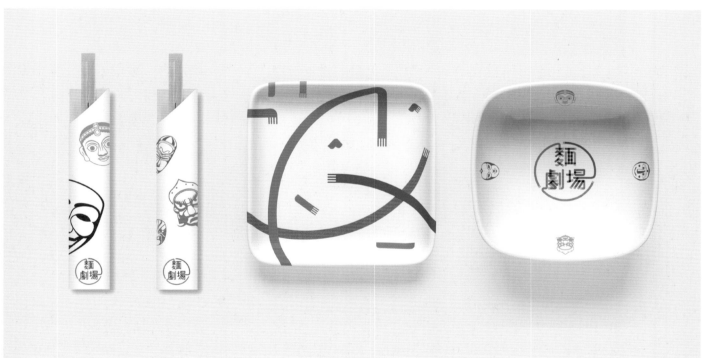

Noodle Theater is a restaurant chain in Taiwan serving regional noodle dishes from around the globe. The identity features a bold color palette that alludes to the restaurant's multicultural offerings and diversity of ingredients. The colorful identity extends to a series of ethnic masks, including a Mexican luchador mask, a Japanese noh mask, and a British Guy Fawkes mask, each representing a unique culture.

**Studio: Pentagram**

# The Lodhi

The hotel Lodhi is located in the heart of Delhi's cultural heritage. The rebranding aspired to underline the hotel's recreation services and standards of excellence. As the hotel name suggests, the identity design adopted its theme from medieval India's Lodhi dynasty. The logo and the department symbols have intertwined custom patterns and motifs of the era with various aspects of the design, resonating with the opulence of Indian heritage.

**Studio: Green Goose Design**

GYMNASIUM

POOL CAFÉ

SPA

BAKERY

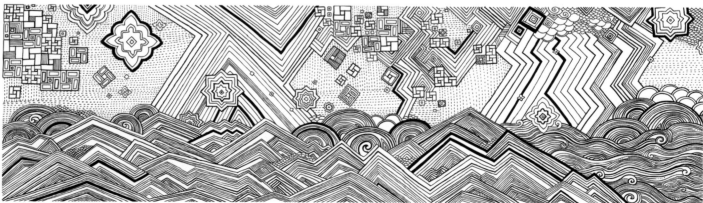

# Xu Xiaoming TCM Surgical Clinic

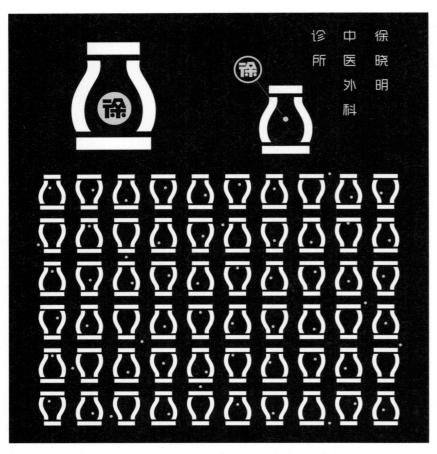

徐晓明
中医外科
诊所

Based on the demands in two aspects of "professional treatment" and "daily health product development", three core elements have been abstracted for the branding: the "elixir vitae" suggesting the wisdom of traditional Chinese medicine; the "alchemy furnace", a container indicating the Oriental wisdom; a symbol of Xu Family who is the inheritor of such wisdom. The connection between these elements is "refinement", which refers not only to the alchemy, but also the pursuit of good health and longevity by the Orientals.

**Studio: 1983ASIA**
**Creative Director: Susu & Yao**
**Designer: Susu & Yao, Kip Lau, Feng Liang**

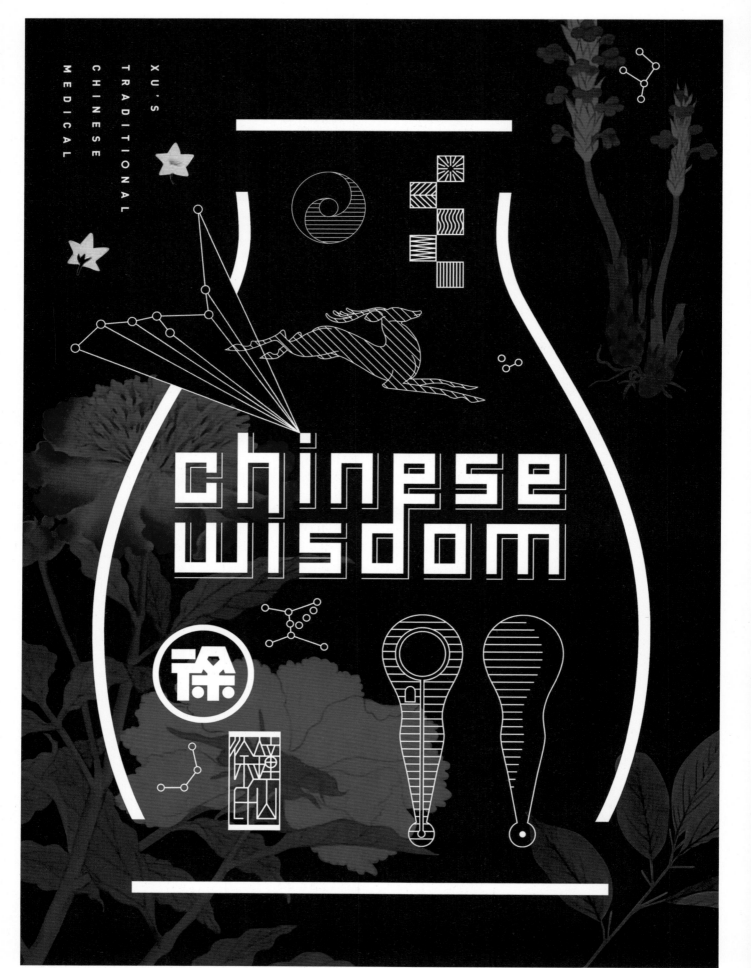

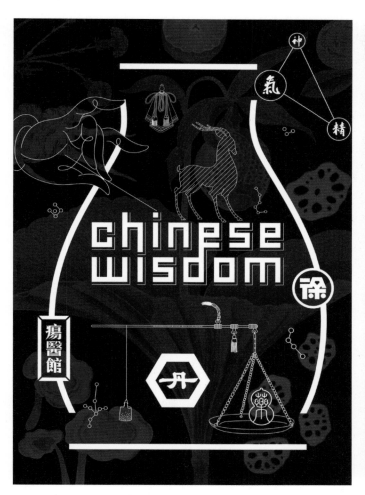

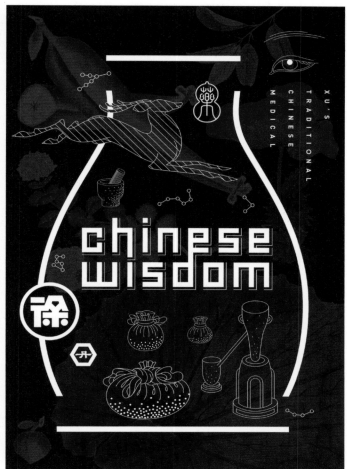

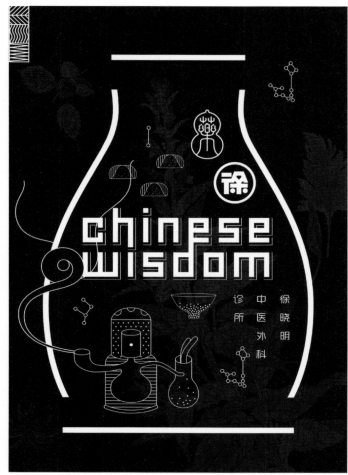

# Qoniki

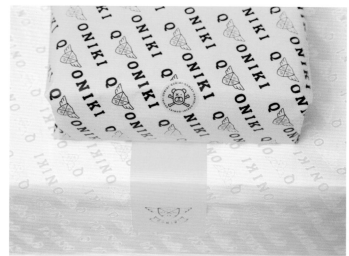

Qoniki is an urban multi-brand sneaker and apparel store for kids. The aim was to create a fun, cool and hip branding that would appeal to kids from 5 to 12 years old and differ from other brands. The shield logo and different icons were created, such as the Bad Teddy and Rebel Rabbit, to underline the rebellious side of kids.

**Designer: Ipek Eris**
**Photographer: Enis Berksoy**

# Stash

Stash is a premium razor supply company. Inspired by the colors and dizzy patterns of the barber's pole, the identity design brings us back to a time when a man took pride in the superior quality and refinement of his appearance. Each of the 24 products is represented by a unique flag symbol.

**Studio: YesYou   Designer: Eric Nishioka**

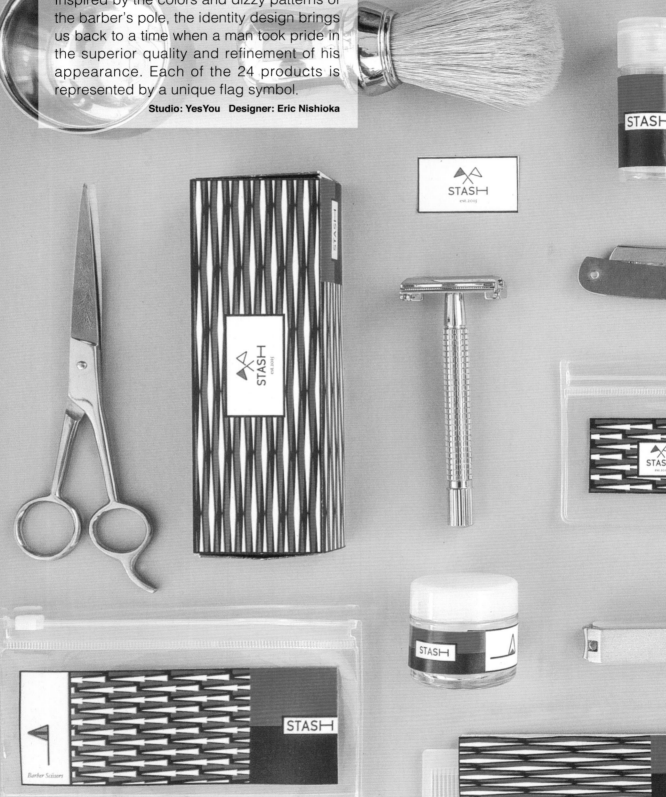

# STASH

## est.2015

### Fine Shaving Products

Razor

Razor Delxe

Saftey Razor

Single Edge

Double Edge

Quad Edge

Cartridge Deluxe

4" Comb

Double Pick

Barber Scissors

Foaming Gel

Straight Razor

Razor Refils

Clippers

Brush Bowl

Shave Brush

After Shave

Stash Wax

Lotion

Stash Bag

Stash is a premium razor supply company for those that demand uncompromised excellence. Inspired by the colors and dizzy patterns of the barber's pole, the brand harkens back to a time when a man could took pride in the the superior quality and refinement of ones appreance. Available for professionals and home care shaving needs, you will find that every encounter with Stash Products will leave you looking as sharp as the blades they produce.

All Rights Reserved     Established in 2015     Los Angeles, CA

STASH

# Echigo Tsurukame Seasonal Sake

For the label design, simplified symbols of crane and tortoise are used to illustrate the brand name and to symbolize auspiciousness and longevity. The package also presents the seasonal sake series through differentiated color scheme to deliver a distinctive visual as well as tasting experience for each season.

**Designer: Kuroyanagi Jun**

# Before & After

Most of the symbols found in traditional Chinese wedding are deemed unfashionable due to its bold and direct artistic treatments. This project aims to explore contemporary interpretations of their auspicious connotations without losing the original values and symbolism. Intricate treatments had been applied in harmonious proportions in an attempt to introduce a new perspective towards traditional Chinese wedding customary products.

**Designer: Cheryl Tan**

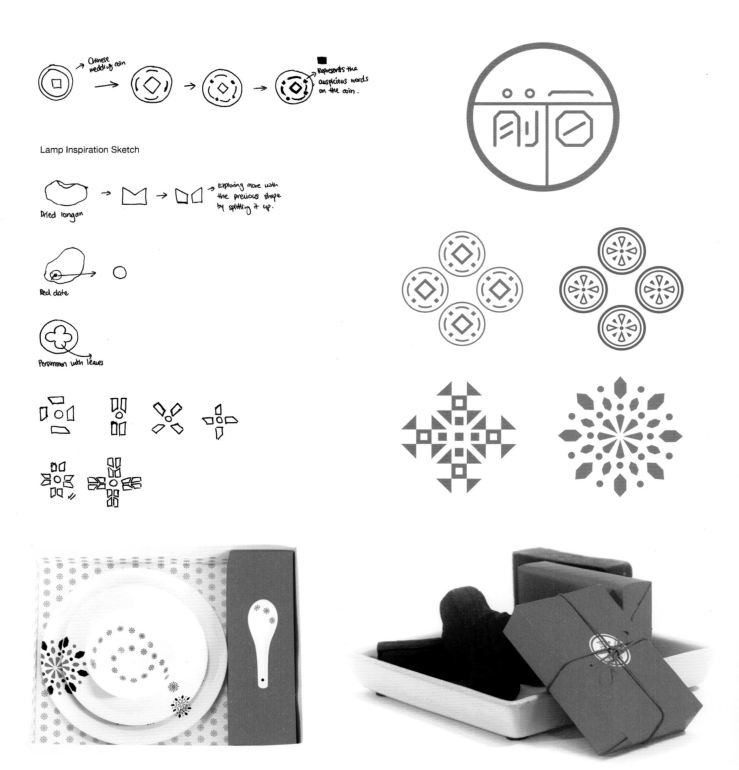

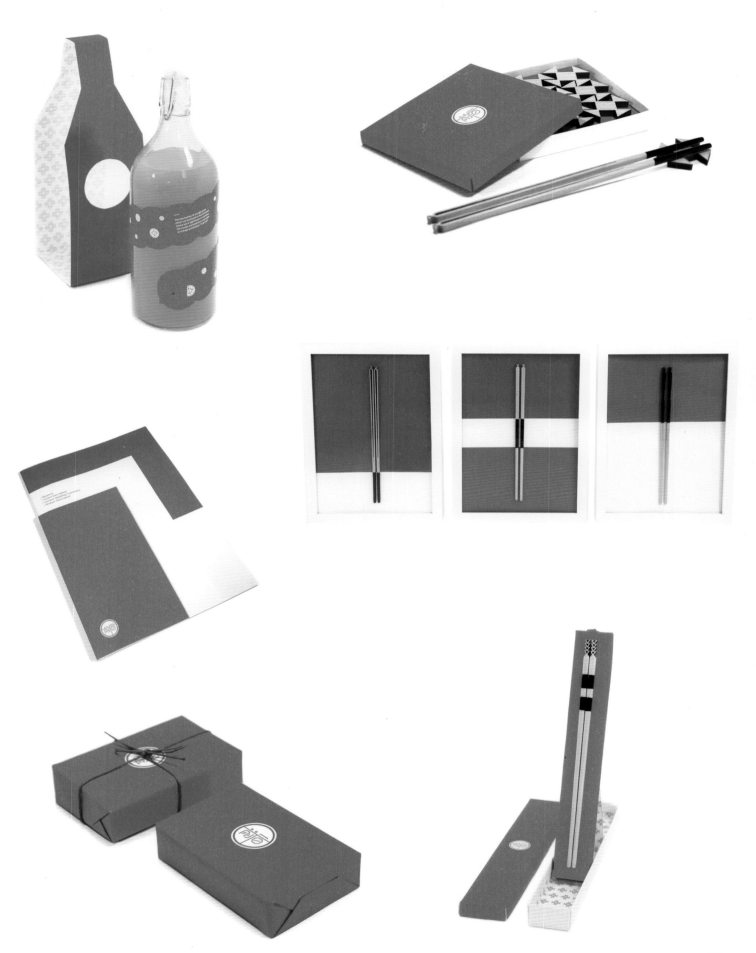

# Asif—Make Sake Project

The crowdfunding project "Make Sake Project" allows the participants experience the making of a type of sake called asif in a long-established brewery. The purpose of this project is to promote a new way of enjoying Japanese sake in a time when its consumption is going down, not just by "drinking" it, but also through "experience". On the bottle strip label are four symbols that respectively represent "traditional sake brewery", "sake brewer", "rice", and "water", the essential elements of asif.

**Studio: tegusu Inc.**
**Designer: Masaomi Fujita**

Sakagura

Sake brewer

Rice

Water

# asif.

MAKE SAKE PROJECT

飯沼本家 asif 2016 ［純米吟醸酒］

# Mustilli

Mustilli is a time-honored wine company in Sant'Agata de' Goti, Italy. The label design for the wine bottles has been injected with representative elements of the territory and its history: the Isclero river water, the pyramidal Ariella hill, the Sant'Agata's crown and the bridge that crosses the medieval hamlet. Then each symbol is complemented by the Mustilli family icon: the shield.

**Studio: nju:comunicazione**

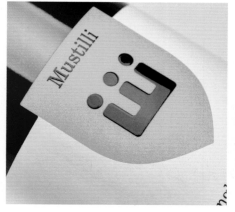
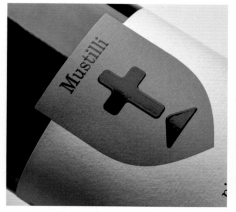
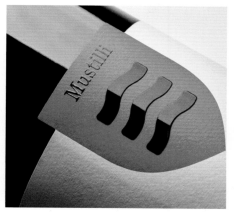

# Christmas Survival Kit

Christmas Survival Kit is a little package of gifts sent out to the studio's important retailers to help them get through the busy month of December. Each kit includes some festive essentials and Christmas comforts, all snuggly packaged in a box reminiscent of a medical first aid kit. To complete the image, the classic Red Cross symbol has been redesigned to communicate the playful character.

**Studio: Suck UK**
**Photographer: Enrico Policardo**

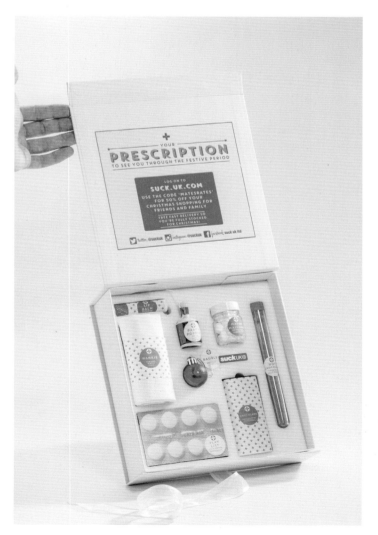

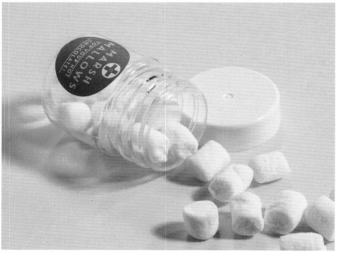

# Cacao Cultura

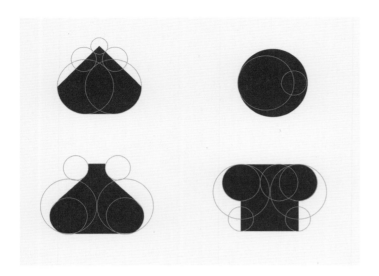

Cacao Cultura is a brand initiated by Kvorum Agency, one of Russia's largest chocolate distributors. The identity features four different symbols which respectively represent the origins of the organic chocolate—France, Belgium, Switzerland and Russia. These scattered symbols also help construct dynamic and rhythmical compositions for the layout, made out of different types of foils to create an association with the confectionary wrappers.

**Designer: Vladimir Shlygin**

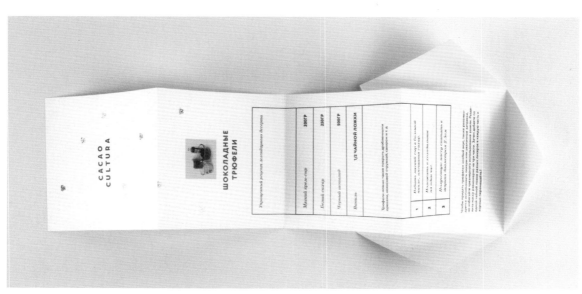

# Demijhon Beer

The visual representation in the branding conveys the product's excellence—being concocted in a laboratory with extensive knowledge and professional tools. The color scheme represents the laboratory atmosphere: the light cream color for cleanness and sterilization, the black for machines and the orange for the safety signs.

**Designer: Ifat Zexer**

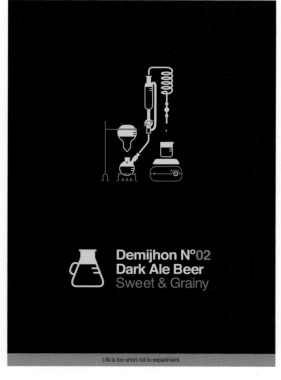

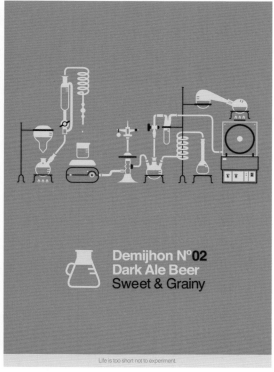

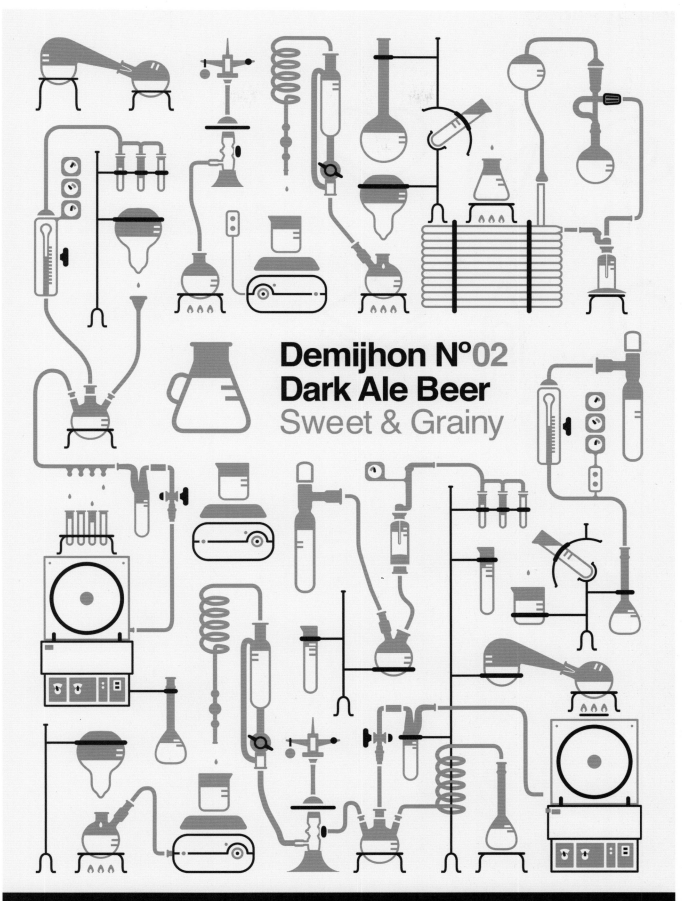

# Demijhon N°02
# Dark Ale Beer
## Sweet & Grainy

# Design Papers

Design Papers is a paper catalog created for Europapier, a paper company targeted at graphic industry professionals for over 40 years. The two decorative groups of pictograms help define the catalog's visual and tactile aspects. The "look, touch and feel" emphasizes the interactive character and the design treatment as an object and packaging. The "carefully created collection" has a gold foil finishing and emphasizes the outstanding quality.

**Studio: Metaklinika**
**Creative Director: Nenad Trifunović, Lazar Bodroža**
**Art Director: Nenad Trifunović**
**Designer: Ivan Kostić**

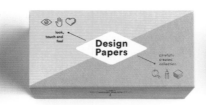
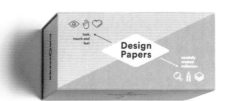

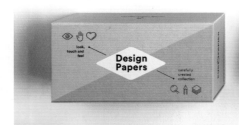

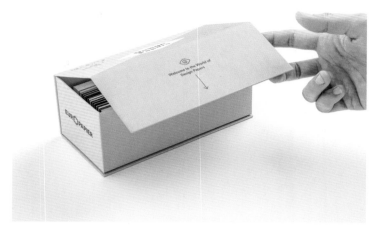

# A Royal Letterhead

The stationery set features a consistent set of symbols based on traditional Ghanaian royal culture. The classic symbol of West African Sankofa bird is an emblem suggesting learning from your past to better understand your future. The crossed swords are Akrafena, an Ashanti sword used for Ghana's national sport. The mask symbol refers to the traditional Ashanti beaded stools that are usually made from sese wood. Last but not least, the crest with a fire breathing dog is a symbol of the Aduana clan.

**Studio: ONOGRIT Designstudio**
**Designer: Daniela Kempkes, Alix Hopfengaertner-Vigneault, Janina Braun**

# Local Food Package Design

This package design aims to promote local food consumption and nature protection. Some graphic symbols were created based on the universally recognized prohibition sign and the long distance transportation, while the key symbol of a bicycle topped with an apple suggests short distance trip and environmental friendliness.

**Designer: Kwag Yeon-jung**

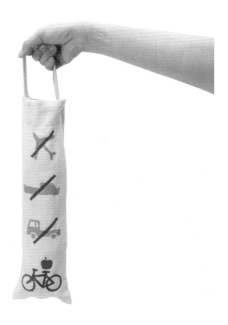

# Puebla 109

Being a restaurant, a bar and members club, Puebla 109 is a three-story 20th century townhouse where art, design and gastronomy converge. The identity was developed around several symbols that drew inspiration from the classic age of Mexican philately and make up a rigid graphic system. The applications stand out with bold colors and classic typefaces that have a strong national character, along with other graphic elements that resemble those used by the postal system in the past.

**Studio: Savvy Studio**
**Photographer: Coke Bartrina**

# Ekies

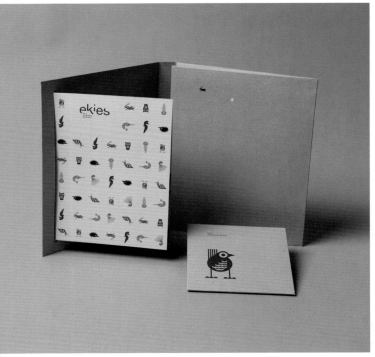

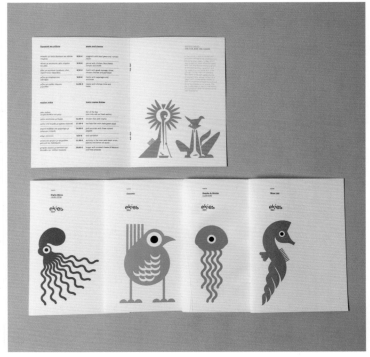

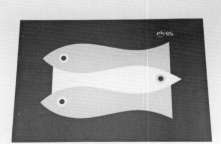

Ekies is a boutique hotel with a contemporary eco-philosophy that lies in a unique natural setting near Vourvourou Bay, Greece. In order to communicate the resort's immersion in the Greek nature, the studio illustrated some local animals as the symbolic elements for the identity.

**Studio: BeetRoot Design Group**

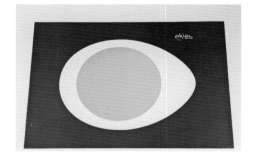

# Biscottini

A package design for biscuits with six different flavors—ginger, apricot oat, raisin oat, sesame, hazelnut, and sea salted cocoa.

**Designer: Akiko Masunaga**

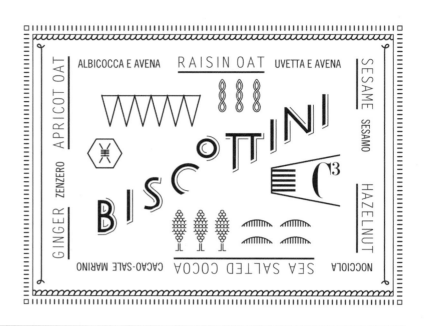

# Cartography of Emotions

Cartography of Emotions is a project that aims to interpret human emotions with colors and shapes, since a lot of people are having problems expressing their feelings with words. According to the psychology of colors and shapes, different symbols are assigned to different types of feeling. For instance, emotions related to happiness are expressed through circular shape and color yellow which together show vitality and optimism. The outcome of the project is totally subjective and personal.

**Designer: Cristina Gomez Garcia**

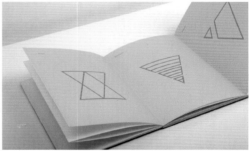

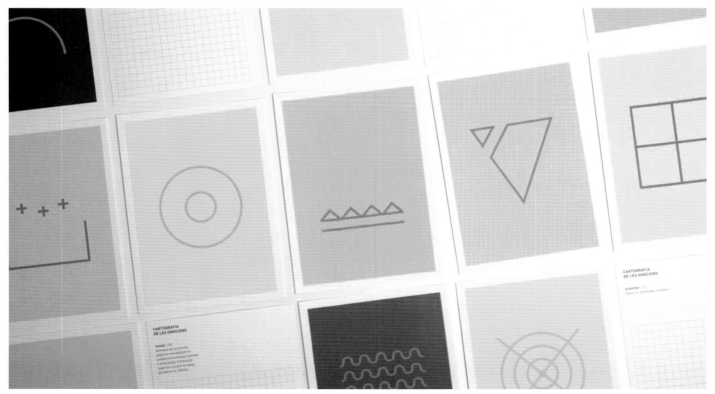

**Michael Goodman**
Manager

St. Joseph Boulevard
1426, Block B/10
New York / NY

C: (135) 578 1455
T: (212) 835 4000
F: (212) 835 4011

goodman@rrpublishhouse.com
www.rrpublishhouse.com

St. Joseph Boulevard
1426, Block B/10
New York / NY

T: (212) 835-4000
F: (212) 835-4011

info@rrpublishhouse.com
www.rrpublishhouse.com

St. Joseph Boulevard
1426, Block B/10
New York / NY

T: (212) 835-4000
F: (212) 835-4011

info@rrpublishhouse.com
www.rrpublishhouse.com

**VITA SINE LIBRIS MORS EST**
LIFE WITHOUT BOOKS IS DEATH

**Remus** and **Romulus** were twin brothers. They were abandoned by their parents as babies and put into a basket that was then placed into the River Tiber. The basket ran aground and the twins were discovered by a female wolf. The wolf nursed the babies for a short time before they were found by a shepherd. The shepherd then brought up the twins.When Romulus and Remus became adults, they decided to found a city where the wolf had found them. The brothers quarrelled over where the site

should be. But after they decide where to build up their city, Remus was killed by his brother. This left Romulus the sole founder of the new city and he gave his name to it. The date given for the founding of **Rome is 753 BC.**

For More Information
www.rrpublishhouse.com

R&R
Remus & Romulus
Publish House

St. Joseph Boulevard
1426, Block 8/10
New York / NY

T: (212) 835-4000
P: (212) 835-4011

info@rrpublishhouse.com
www.rrpublishhouse.com

R&R
Remus & Romulus
Publish House

R&R
Remus & Romulus
Publish House

St. Joseph Boulevard
1426, Block 8/10
New York / NY

T: (212) 835-4000
F: (212) 835-4011

info@rrpublishhouse.com
www.rrpublishhouse.com

VIVA ENIM MORTUORUM IN MEMORIA VIVORUM EST POSITA
THE LIFE OF THE DEAD IS RETAINED IN THE MEMORY OF THE LIVING

# Remus & Romulus

Remus & Romulus is a publishing house which took its name from the mythical twin brother founders of Ancient Rome. The story of the founding of Rome gives a historical feeling towards the brand image. Accordingly, a symbol was illustrated based on the famous Capitoline Wolf sculpture closely related to this dark and bloody story.

**Designer: Berk Büyüksezer**
**Photographer: Ali Can Toygar**

# Emmanuelle

Emmanuelle is a crew of film makers who named their team in reference to the French mythic erotic movies from the 1970s. The whole brief was about femininity but nor girly, sexiness with delicacy, and sensibility with strength.

**Studio: Violaine & Jérémy**

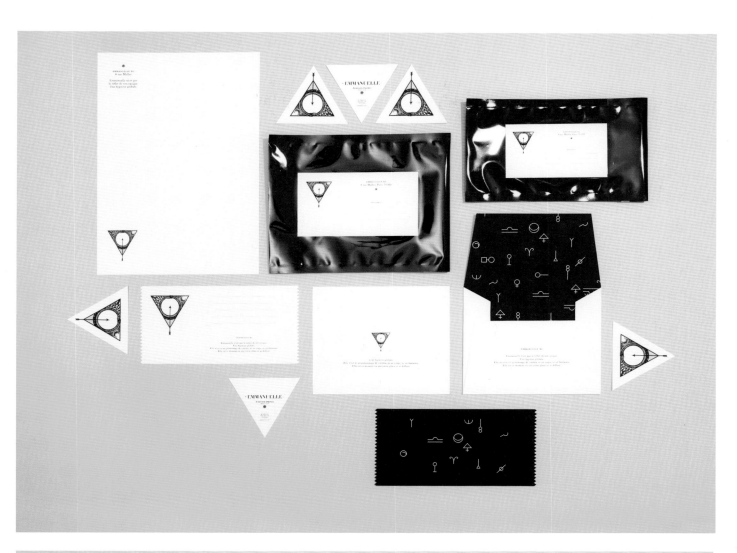

# Devoto

**MUŽ A ŽENA**

Men and Women

**SVOBODA**

Freedom

**DÉŠŤ**

Rain

**MOUDROST**

Wisdom

**HORY**

Mountain

**HAD**

Snake

**KUKUŘICE**

Corn

**DÍTĚ**

Child—Father's Pride

**RYBY**

Fish

**SILNÝ LÉK**

Strong Medicine

**VÝCHOD SLUNCE**

Sunrise

**MEDVĚD**

Bear

**DEN**

Day

**KŮŇ**

Horse

Based on the theme of American Indian, illustrations along with the typical symbols were created for the children accessories, in hope that the children could play and learn with fun.

**Illustrator: Patrik Antczak**

SILNÝ LĖK

VESNICE

VÁLEČNÍCI NA KÁNOI

# Smile Gallery

Smile gallery is a humorous pop-up store for the leader of invisible orthodontics, Invisalign, developed around the concept of "taking life with smile". Various smile related symbols, like the upward curved lips and smiley, created for the interior hold the key of the visual expression. They are the embodiment of emotions.

**Studio: M&C Saatchi Little Stories**
**Creative Director: Christophe Burine**
**Art Director: Lise Armand**
**Illustrator: Jean-Michel Tixier**

# Loot

Loot is a surf and lifestyle store in Zihuatanejo, Mexico, offering an interesting alternative to the commercial options commonly found in a touristic location. The brand's personality and graphic identity combine historical elements of the region with modern pop culture: the graphic language was conceived around treasure hunts and pirate maps, like the X that marks spot. And the neutral color palette was meant to highlight the individual objects within the store.

**Studio: Savvy Studio**

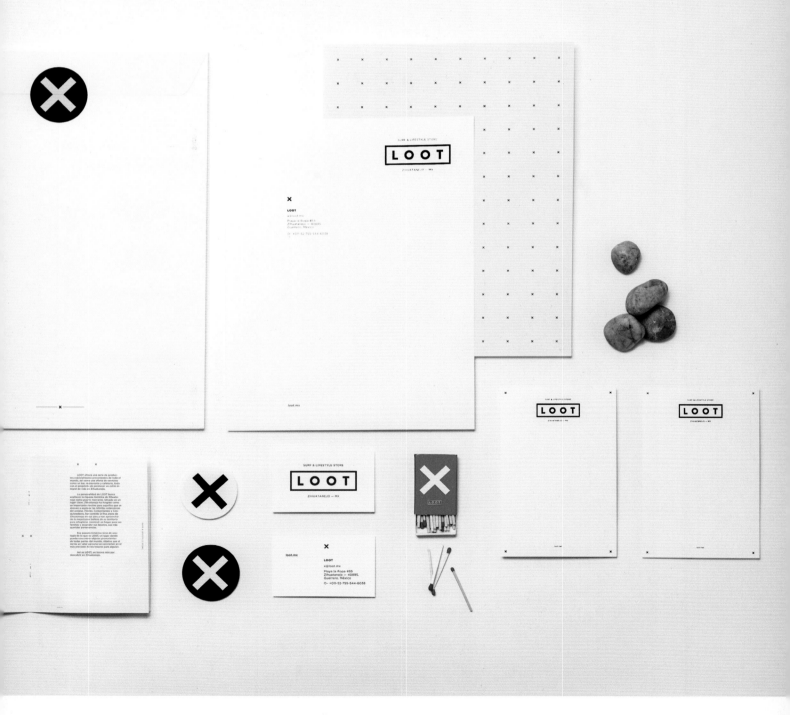

# Your Interface

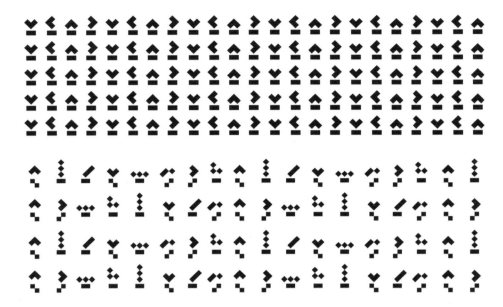

Your Interface is a marketing and communication agency based on two essential values—science and creativity. The five symbols in the identity were formed by an arrowhead and a rectangle, referring to the Y and I letters. The horizontal rectangle symbolizes a strong foundation and accuracy while the arrowhead responsiveness and flexibility.

**Designer: Michał Markiewicz**
**Supervision: Your Interface**

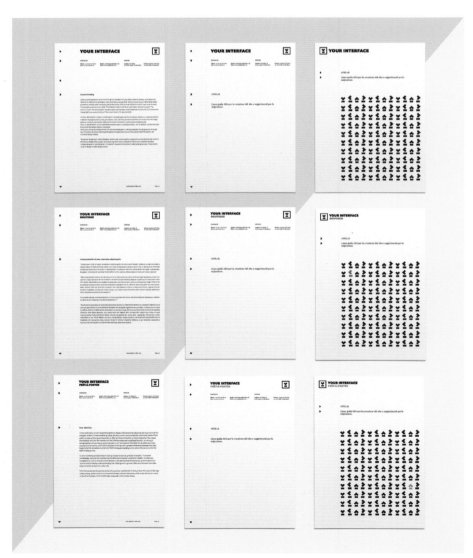

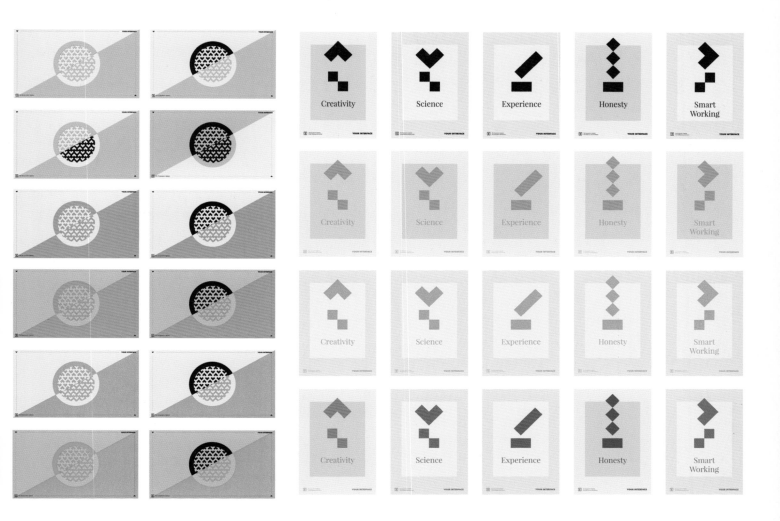

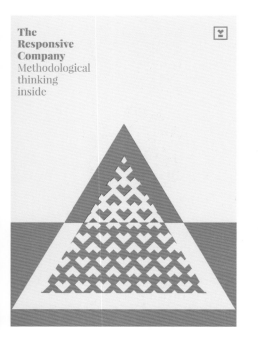

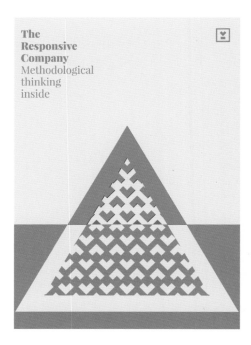

# Gbox Studios

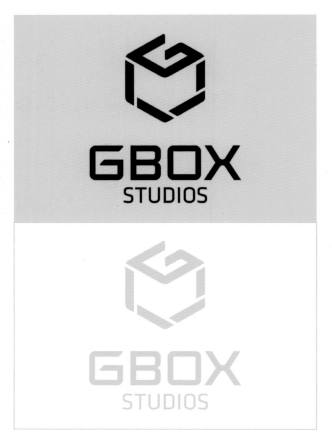

Gbox is an advertising photography and video production studio. A series of symbols have been added to the identity to reflect the brand's characters and core values, arranged with the alphabetic characters of the brand name to form a highly flexible layout.

**Studio: Bratus**
**Photographer: Eric Huynh**

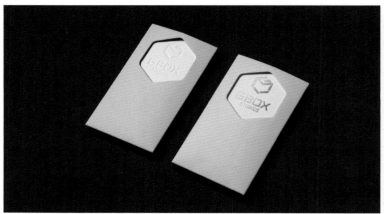

EXPLORE CREATE INSPIRE

# Hands

Hands is a live marketing agency. The concept of "handmade ideas" has been the agency's philosophy. Apart from a series of hand shape symbols, the emblem of pentagon surrounding the letter H was created to symbolize the five fingers of a hand.

**Studio: P/P Studio**
**Designer: Pedro Paulino**

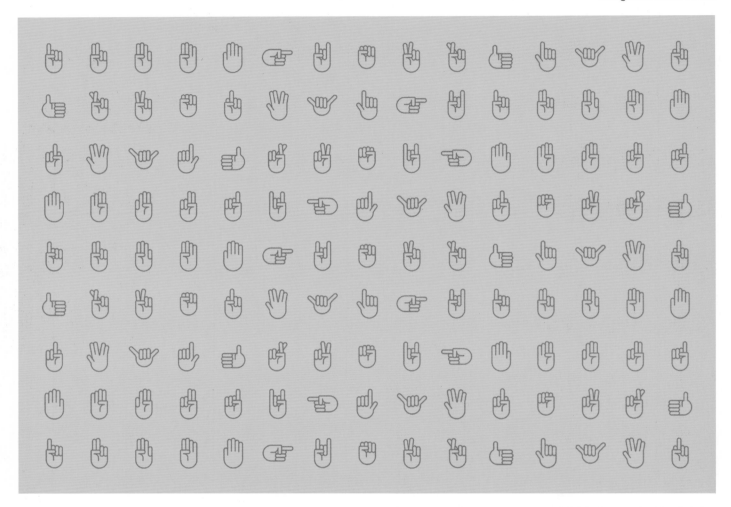

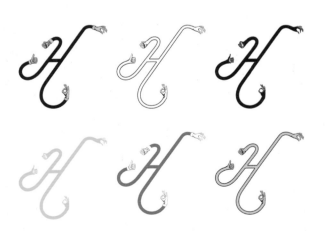

# Arcadia Data

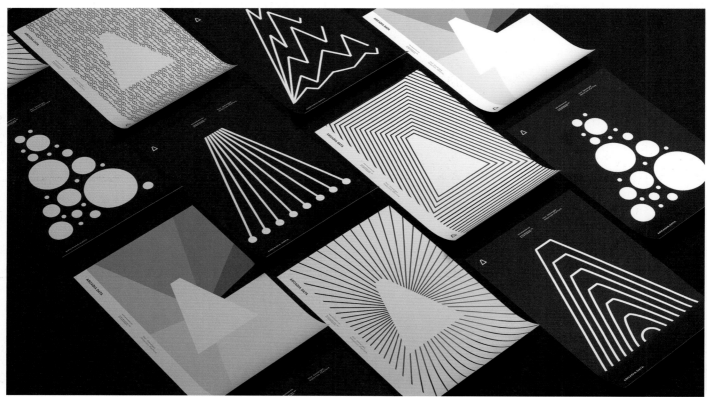

Different A-shaped symbols have been created in a clean and smart way to show that Arcadia Data translates raw information into something meaningful, compelling and personal. The designer reified these simple shapes by applying negative space, filled space, 2D, 3D, closure and more under the Gestalt laws of grouping. The symbols can be improvised and placed throughout almost any brand touch point.

**Designer: Casey Martin**
**Illustrator: Casey Martin**
**Animator: Brent Clouse, Jonathan Corriveau**
**Photographer: Jonathan Corriveau, Eric Louis Haines**

# Emmaroz

MÉRETES NŐI
SZABÓSÁG & SZALON

szeged

**Emmaroz**

MÉRETES NŐI
SZABÓSÁG & SZALON

SZEGED

**Szénási Enikő Lilla**

*ügyvezető*
*fashion director*

+ 36 30 958 9996
eniko.szenasi@emmaroz.moda
www.emmaroz.moda

**Szénási Enikő Lilla**

*ügyvezető*
*fashion director*

+ 36 30 958 9996
eniko.szenasi@emmaroz.moda
www.emmaroz.moda

**Szénási Enikő Lilla**

*ügyvezető*
*fashion director*

+ 36 30 958 9996
eniko.szenasi@emmaroz.moda
www.emmaroz.moda

**emmaroz**

CUT & SEW

CONTRACTOR

**Ildikó Madarász**

*Heaf of Sales*

+ 36 30 681 7615
ildiko.madarasz@emmaroz.moda
www.emmaroz.moda

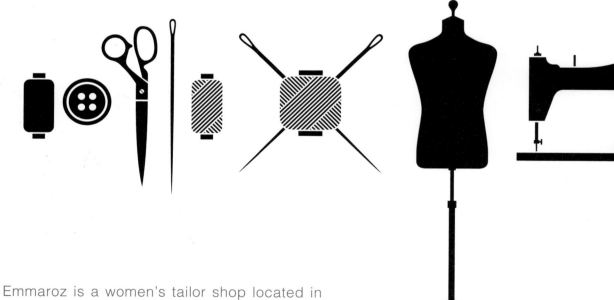

Emmaroz is a women's tailor shop located in Szeged, Hungary. Many tailoring-related items have been transformed into striking symbols for the identity. Some small details of classic fashion style echo the femininity, purity, and salon atmosphere of the interior design.

**Designer: kissmiklos**
**Photographer: Balint Jaksa**

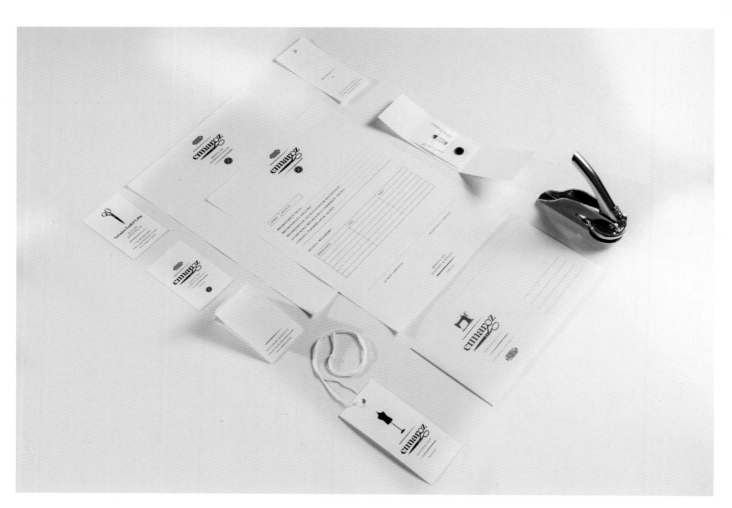

# Saint-Étienne Opera House

OPÉRA|THÉÂTRE DE SAINT-ÉTIENNE

2006

OPERATHEATRE
◆ SAINTETIENNE ◆

2012

ⵔPĔRA
SAINT-ÉTIENNE

2015

THE ROOF

É

THE HALL

THE SCENE

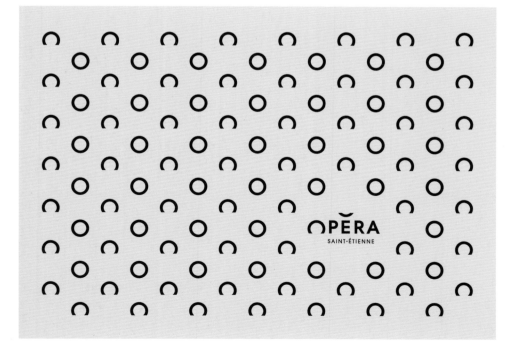

The objective of the branding was to establish a sense of closeness with the people of Saint-Étienne Opera House through simple and down-to-earth communication. In the logo, the accent on top of the letter E increases the intensity of voice and resembles the building's curved rooftop, while the shape of the "O" brings to mind an open mouth singing an operatic aria. The accent and the letter O have been developed into key visuals to create dynamics of music and dance in the opera.

**Studio: Graphéine**

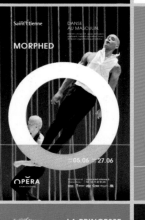

# Backside Calendar

Backside Calendar was created to promote the studio's creative services. Playing on the sex appeal of "butts" to attract attention, the designer whimsically illustrates how every month offers its own significant "butt" moment. Taking traditional Chinese festivals, cultural, religious, social and even local political events as its inspiration, the minimalist yet multi-faceted calendar leaves all to the eye of the beholder to enjoy.

**Studio: Toby Ng Design**
**Creative Director: Toby Ng**
**Designer: Toby Ng, Ronald Cheung**

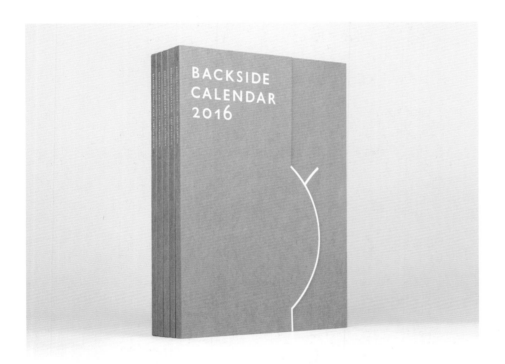

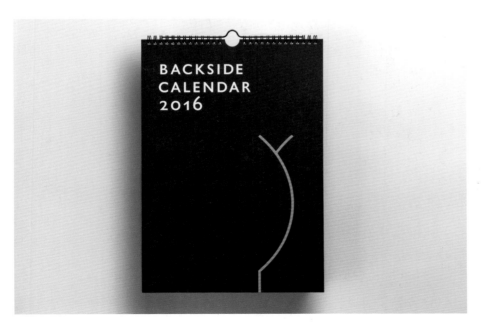

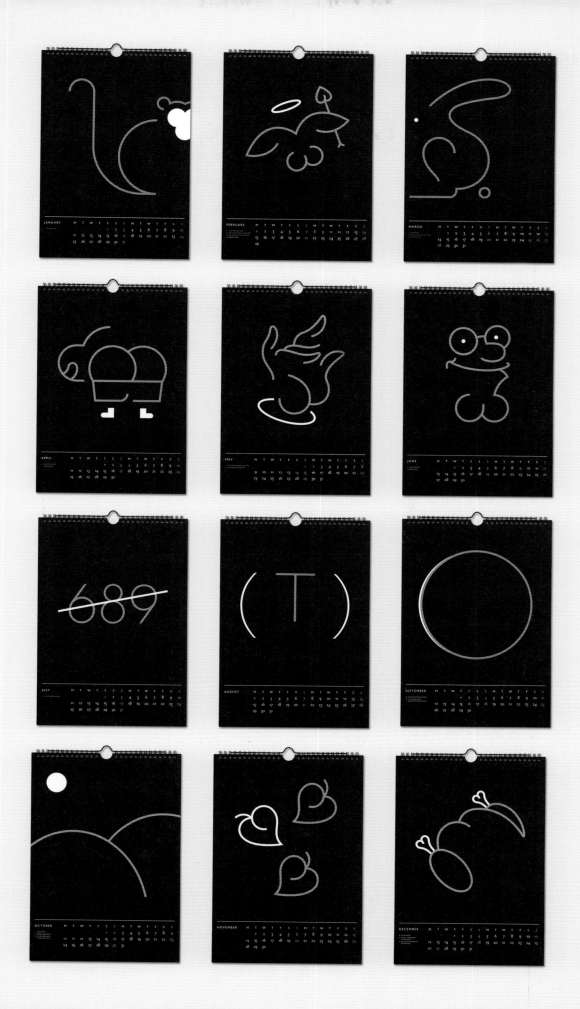

# The Dreslyn Tarot

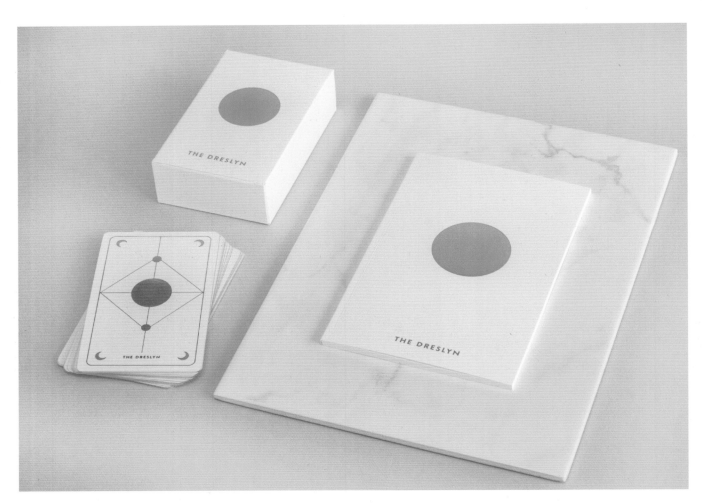

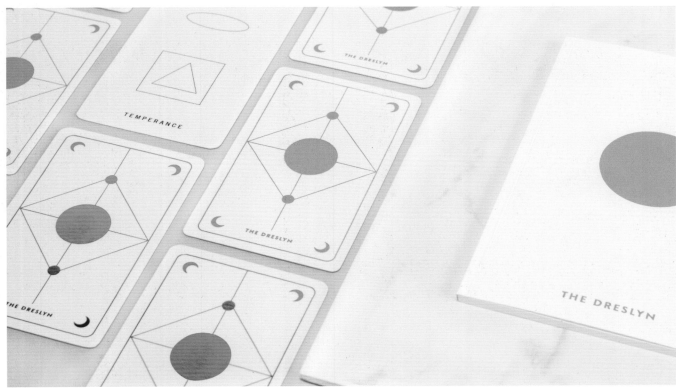

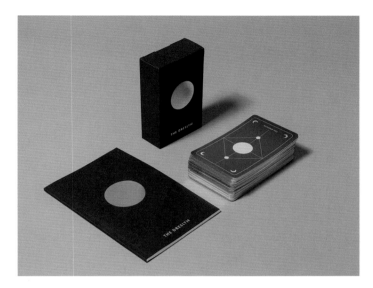

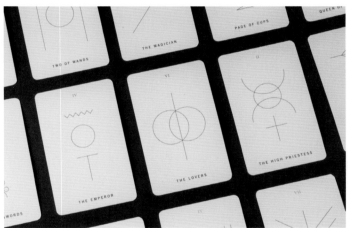

In contrast to the conventional ornate and complex illustrations, the designer has created a series of Tarot cards that combines the minimalist aesthetics with the intuitive art of Tarot, using only hairline shapes and as few shapes as possible to get across the idea or concept of all the 78 cards.

**Designer: Kati Forner**

World Children's Festival celebrates creativity in young imaginative minds, encouraging exploration, collaboration and unity. The new identity reflects these values and gives a unique ownership to the attending children. The logo and symbols are at the heart of the brand's reconfiguration, through which the children can make their own symbols by remixing the existing ones, or drawing on top of the logo. These symbols are used as pictograms to convey a more visual sense of imagination.

**Studio: Larssen & Amaral**

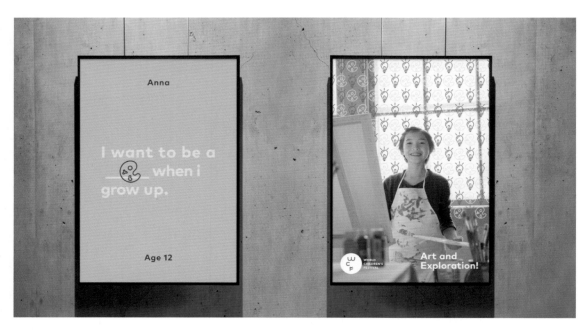

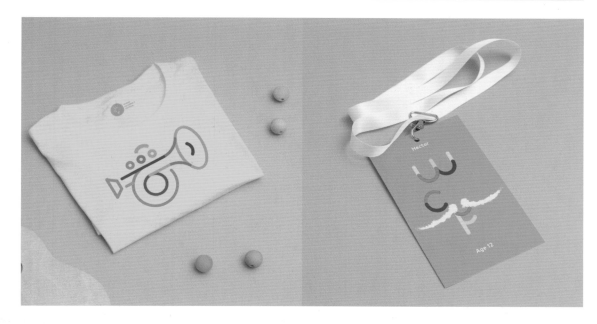

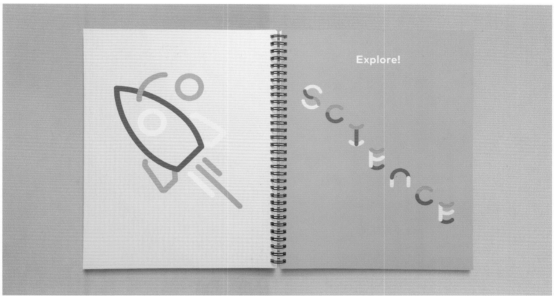

The world 🌐 is a wonderful place. Creativity 🎨 empowers all of us. Peace ☮ and a strong sense of leadership ⚑ encourage our imagination, 💡 healthy 💙 hearts and minds.

# Lilla Hjärtat

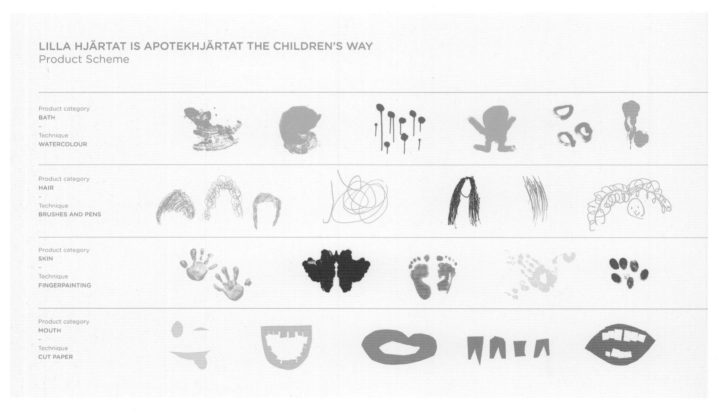

**LILLA HJÄRTAT IS APOTEKHJÄRTAT THE CHILDREN'S WAY**
Product Scheme

Product category
BATH
–
Technique
WATERCOLOUR

Product category
HAIR
–
Technique
BRUSHES AND PENS

Product category
SKIN
–
Technique
FINGERPAINTING

Product category
MOUTH
–
Technique
CUT PAPER

Apotek Hjärtat is one of the largest pharmacy chains in Sweden. The studio developed a concept for Apotek Hjärtat´s child and baby products and named it Lilla Hjärtat (The Little Heart). A series of patterns created by children were used as the key visuals to symbolize different products.

**Studio: Bold**

# Fasm

fasm®

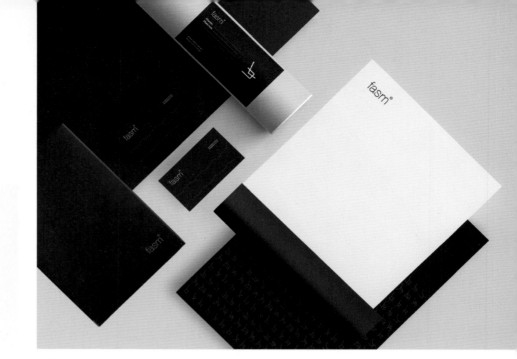

fasm®

FASM is a brand dedicated to the area of furniture and other product design. Different chair symbols have been developed for the branding based on some chair models from the brand and some iconic pieces in history, in a minimalist design language that the brand follows.

**Studio: Bullseye**

# Mandarin Natural Chocolate

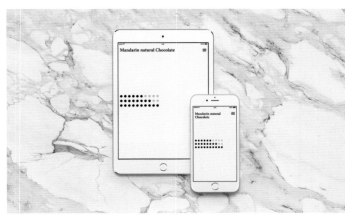

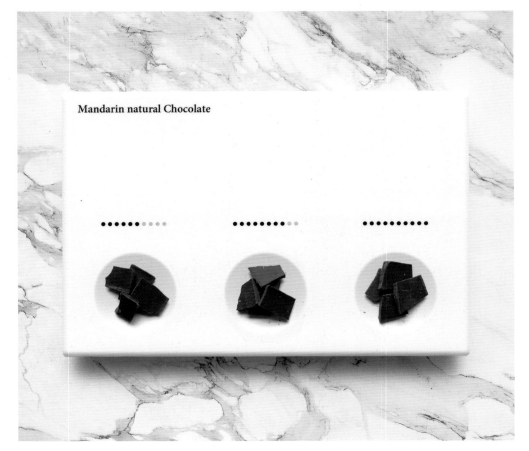

Mandarin natural Chocolate offers 60%, 80% and 100% cacao chocolate bars made from organic cacao and cane sugar. A line of 10 dots has been an important symbolic element throughout the branding, subtly indicating the chocolate intensity. Every single black dot represents 10% of cacao in the mixture.

**Designer: Yuta Takahashi**

# Bart

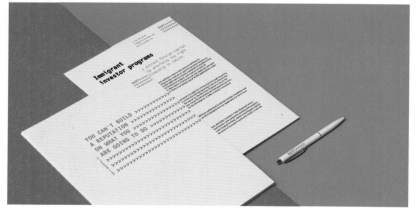

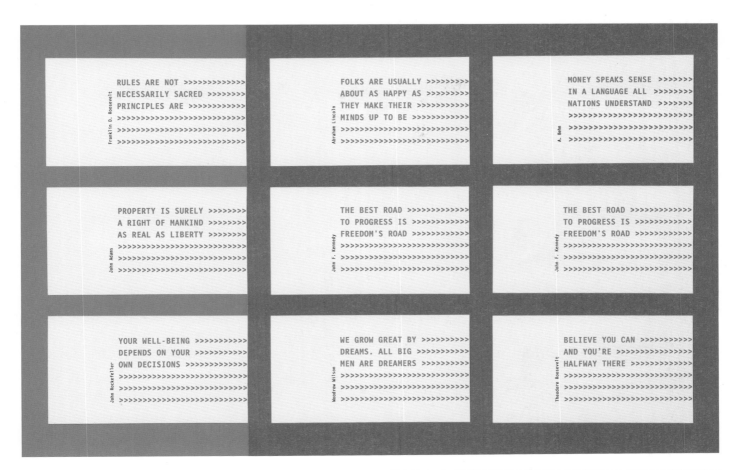

| | |
|---|---|
| **Franklin D. Roosevelt** RULES ARE NOT >>>>>>>>>>> NECESSARILY SACRED >>>>>>> PRINCIPLES ARE >>>>>>>>>> >>>>>>>>>>>>>>>>>>>> >>>>>>>>>>>>>>>>>>>> | **Abraham Lincoln** FOLKS ARE USUALLY >>>>>>>> ABOUT AS HAPPY AS >>>>>>>> THEY MAKE THEIR >>>>>>>>> MINDS UP TO BE >>>>>>>>>> >>>>>>>>>>>>>>>>>>>> >>>>>>>>>>>>>>>>>>>> |

A bunch of quotes laid out on business cards:

- **Franklin D. Roosevelt** — RULES ARE NOT NECESSARILY SACRED PRINCIPLES ARE
- **Abraham Lincoln** — FOLKS ARE USUALLY ABOUT AS HAPPY AS THEY MAKE THEIR MINDS UP TO BE
- **A. Behn** — MONEY SPEAKS SENSE IN A LANGUAGE ALL NATIONS UNDERSTAND
- **John Adams** — PROPERTY IS SURELY A RIGHT OF MANKIND AS REAL AS LIBERTY
- **John F. Kennedy** — THE BEST ROAD TO PROGRESS IS FREEDOM'S ROAD
- **John F. Kennedy** — THE BEST ROAD TO PROGRESS IS FREEDOM'S ROAD
- **John Rockefeller** — YOUR WELL-BEING DEPENDS ON YOUR OWN DECISIONS
- **Woodrow Wilson** — WE GROW GREAT BY DREAMS. ALL BIG MEN ARE DREAMERS
- **Theodore Roosevelt** — BELIEVE YOU CAN AND YOU'RE HALFWAY THERE

Bart Regional Center is a company attracting foreign investments for the funding of development projects in the US. Investments in the American economy through Bart virtually guarantee the entrepreneurs a green card. Taking this subject as the basis of the identity, the designers combined the arrowheads that substitute blank space in green cards, visas, and passports with the American flag. The star-spangled part was replaced with inspiring quotes to visualize the investors' pursuit of the American Dream. And the classic red and blue colors of the flag were refreshed to be modern and bright.

**Studio: Science Agency**
**Art Director: Pavel Konyukov**
**Designer: Ivan Dovydenko**

# The First Syrah Arts and Heritage Festival

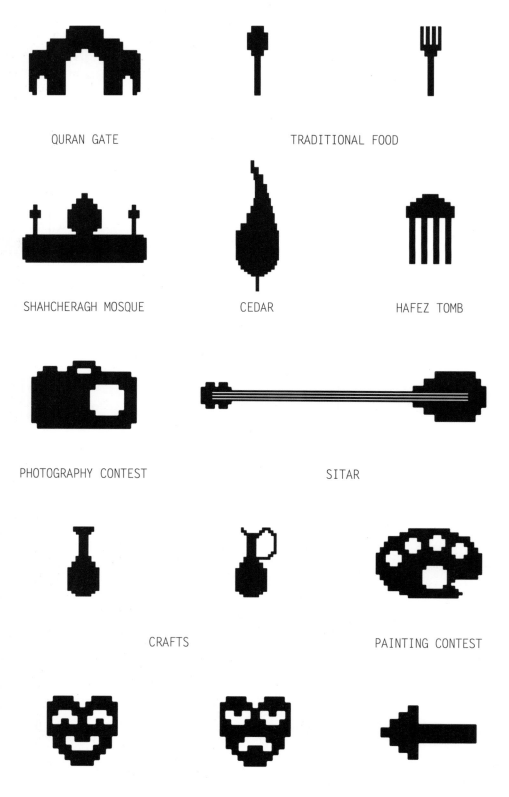

QURAN GATE

TRADITIONAL FOOD

SHAHCHERAGH MOSQUE

CEDAR

HAFEZ TOMB

PHOTOGRAPHY CONTEST

SITAR

CRAFTS

PAINTING CONTEST

THEATRE

ARROW

Syrah is one of the oldest names of Shiraz city. The Syrah Festival includes theatre, painting and architectural contest, etc. The original idea for the identity design was inspired by the cedar tree, a traditional symbol of life in Iran. The other symbols are based on local historical sites and the activities of the festival.

**Art Director: Afshin Ejabat**
**Designer: Farshad Aref-far**
**Photographer: Reza Goorangi**

دفتر تسهیلگری، بهسازی و نوسازی منطقه تاریخی فرهنگی شیراز
و معاونت فرهنگی و امور اجتماعی شهرداری شیراز
با همکاری شرکت عمران و بهسازی شهری ایران برگزار میکنند

## THE FIRST SYRAH ARTS AND HERITAGE FESTIVAL

منطقه تاریخی فرهنگی شیراز میزبان هنر

تئاتر، موسیقی سنتی، عکاسی، هنرهای تجسمی، صنایع دستی، شب شعر، نقد ادبی
مسابقه عکاسی، مسابقه نقاشی، مسابقه اسکچ، فضاسازی شیراز قدیم، غذاهای سنتی شیرازی

از ساعت ۹ صبح لغایت ۷ شب در بافت تاریخی فرهنگی شیراز، محله سنگ سیاه

---

در جست و جوی هویت
فضاهای گمشده شهرم

فراخوان اسکیس در نخستین جشنواره هنر و میراث سیراه
دفتر تسهیلگری، بهسازی و نوسازی منطقه تاریخی فرهنگی شیراز
با همکاری دانشگاه هنر شیراز و انجمن معماران ایران برگزار می کند
افتتاحیه جشنواره: ۹۳/۲/۱۵
زمان برگزاری مسابقه و تحویل آثار: ۹۳/۲/۱۶
اختتامیه و اهدا جوایز: ۹۳/۲/۲۱
از ساعت ۱۰صبح لغایت ۷ بعد از ظهر

---

سایه‌های خشت و خاک

فراخوان نقاشی در نخستین جشنواره هنر و میراث سیراه
دفتر تسهیلگری، بهسازی و نوسازی منطقه تاریخی فرهنگی شیراز
با همکاری انجمن هنرهای تجسمی و سنتی فارس برگزار می کند
افتتاحیه جشنواروآغاز مسابقه: ۹۳/۲/۱۵ تحویل آثار:۹۳/۲/۱۹
داوری آثار:۹۳/۲/۲۰ اختتامیه و اهدا جوایز:۹۳/۲/۲۱
از ساعت ۱۰صبح لغایت ۷ بعد از ظهر

# OFFF Festival

The OFFF Festival is a post-digital era festival. The new visual applications have been enriched by symbols derived from the geometric shapes of the logo, which work as part of the signage of the event and represent the different layers of the event as well as all the disciplines involved. Collectively the symbols are an extension of the brand's nature—movement, dynamism, geometry, and creativity.

**Studio: CROWD Studio**
**Designer: Carles Moré**

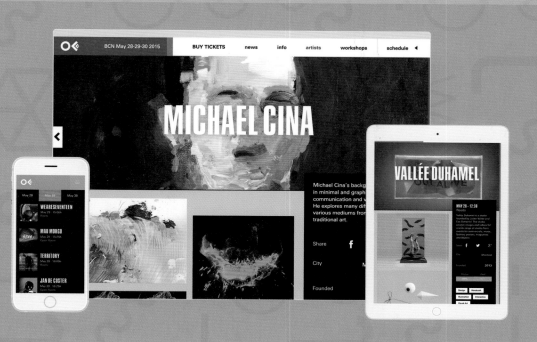

# DOTO

DOTO is an electric power company with more than 50 years of history. The designer created a minimalistic and timeless symbol for the new branding as a visual milestone that marks the next 50 years. The red line symbolizes the wall that DOTO has to get over every day, while the color symbolizes the spirit of Japan and the passion of a conqueror.

**Studio: enhanced Inc.**
**Designer: Hiromi Maeo**

Red Line

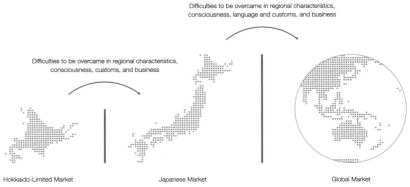

Difficulties to be overcame in regional characteristics, consciousness, language and customs, and business

Difficulties to be overcame in regional characteristics, consciousness, customs, and business

Hokkaido-Limited Market

Japanese Market

Global Market

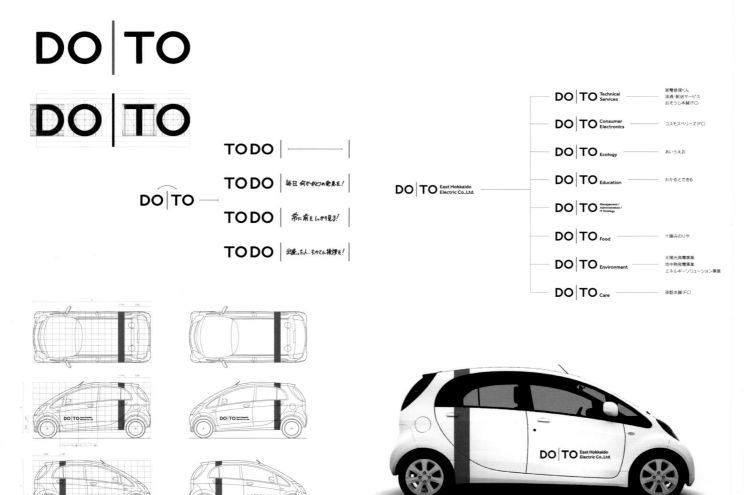

**DO|TO** East Hokkaido Electric Co., Ltd.

**DO|TO** East Hokkaido Electric Co., Ltd.

**DO|TO** East Hokkaido Electric Co., Ltd.

**DO|TO** East Hokkaido Electric Co., Ltd.

**DO|TO** East Hokkaido Electric Co., Ltd.

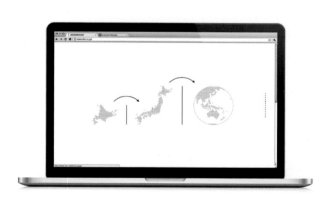

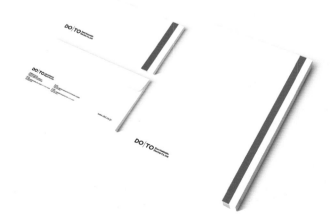

# Johnson & Johnson

 flag, chevron

 golden section foundation

 pulse, health

 oscar, award triumph

 rainbow, peace renovation

 letter, initials

 heart, love

 wheel, progress

 mountain peaks summit

 laurel wreath, victory

 burgeon, birth sprig

 smile, happy

 flag, pennon

 safe, secure calm

 schedule, growth dynamics

 atom, basis molecular model

 flash, beginning generation

For the visuals of Johnson & Johnson's National Sales Meeting, a series of symbols were created to mark the messages being conveyed. Additionally, they formed a compelling typography and build up a simple and clear motion graphic.

**Designer: Alex Frukta, Gleb Koksharov**

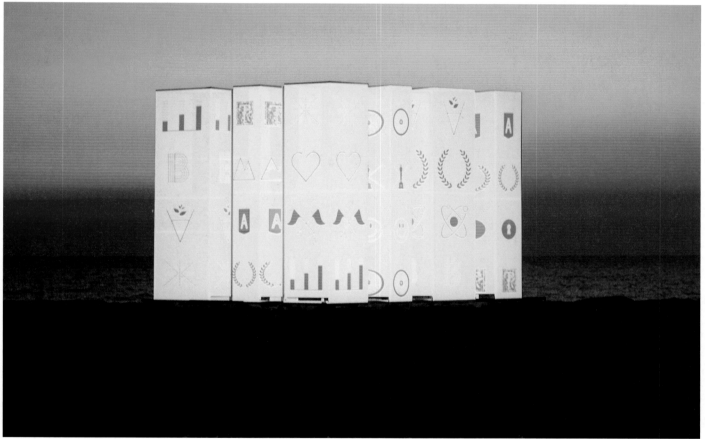

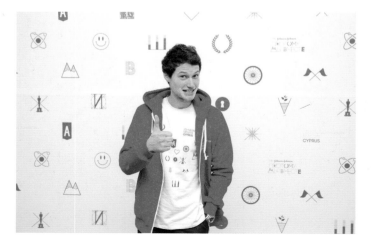

# Coffee Laboratory

The identity for the café is based on puzzle and game. The symbols in the alchemical style indicate the various ingredients of the coffee on sale, and transmit the coffee knowledge through visual code.

**Designer: Sergey Ryadovoy**

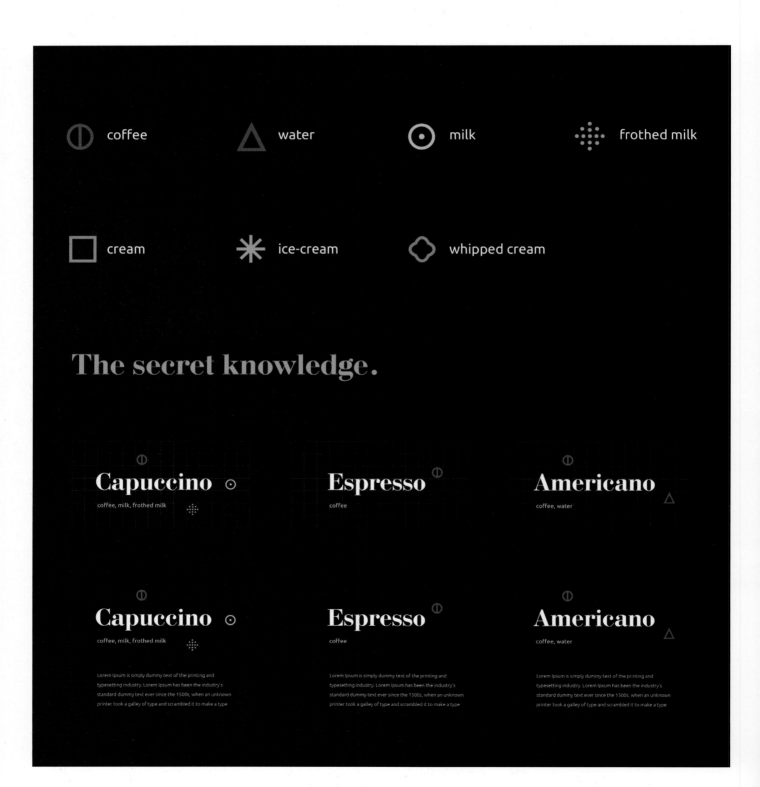

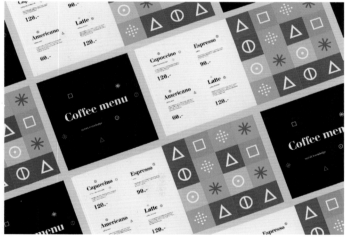

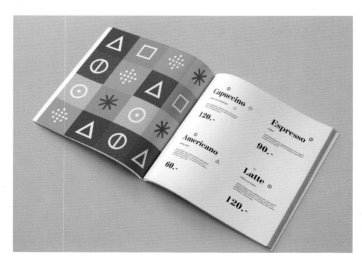

# Identity for the City of Chicago

The sturdy word mark in this identity concept features a tunnel of negative space that carves between letterforms, and was designed to capture a sense of directional, pointed movement and energy. The word mark was dissected into basic geometric shapes which were then combined to form a series of linear patterns that symbolize the city's various municipal departments. Icons built from the same shapes illustrate local events and activities. Using these geometric building blocks to assemble the various patterns and icons provided the consistency and flexibility necessary to represent such a dynamic city.

**Designer: Lauren Howerter**

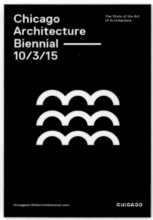

**STREETS AND SANITATION**

**DEPARTMENT OF BUILDINGS**

**POLICE**

**BUREAU OF ARCHITECTURE AND ENGINEERING**

**PLANNING AND DEVELOPMENT**

**WATER MANAGEMENT**

**TRANSIT AUTHORITY**

**INNOVATION AND TECHNOLOGY**

**PUBLIC HEALTH**

---

FULL

CHICAGO

BUREAU OF ARCHITECTURE
AND ENGINEERING

PARTIAL

BUREAU OF ARCHITECTURE
AND ENGINEERING

ABBREVIATED

BAE

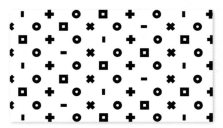
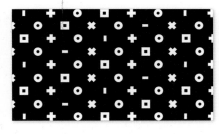
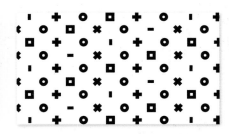

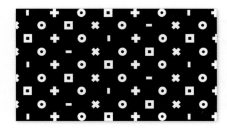
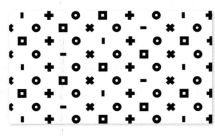
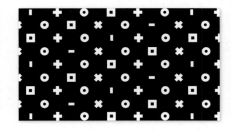

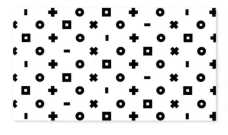
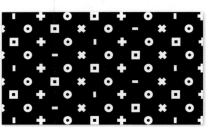

CHICAGO

RAHM EMANUEL
Mayor

121 N LaSalle Street
Chicago City Hall, 4th Floor
Chicago, IL 60602

+1 312 789 8932
remanuel@cityofchicago.org

# The Project Factory

The Project Factory is a digital production company that specializes in innovative and sustainable solutions across online, mobile and gaming space. The branding was inspired by the Rubik's magic cube, reflecting the communication and connections that the company has to offer, as well as alluding to the basic iteration of anything digital: the pixel. A series of symbols and a vibrant color palette produce a dynamic interface visual, and allow the employees to personalize their business cards.

**Studio: Dittmar**
**Designer: Daniel Dittmar**

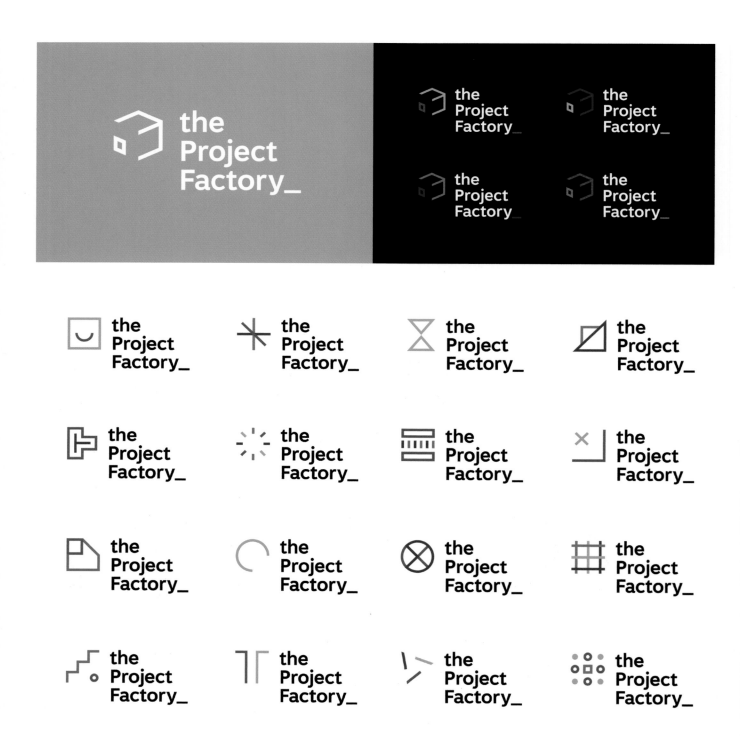

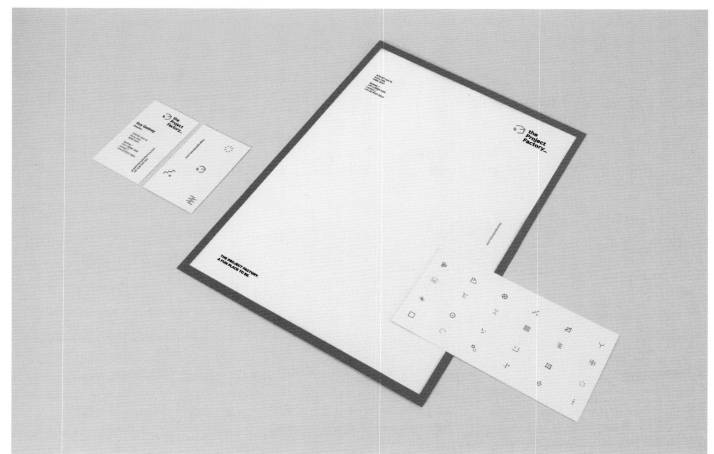

# Uselab

Uselab is a business consulting agency. The identity design is based on the simple and abstract symbols that represent human emotions, a language that is not always understood by everyone. The sea of symbols is a sea of human experiences from which Uselab is able to extract the essence to fulfill their clients' need.

**Studio: Hopa Studio**
**Designer: Norbert Mikolajczyk**

# Mayr Investment Managers

The curves of the trend charts widely used in the finance sector and the wireframes in the architecture have been the main inspirations for the identity when searching for typical symbols and visuals of the finance industry. Lines and grids were eventually formed and positioned in right angles as a representation of the rational decision making process. They also underline the analytical and technology driven work of the client. The logo and the web page correspond with the lines and their positioning in the key visual.

**Designer: Moby Digg**

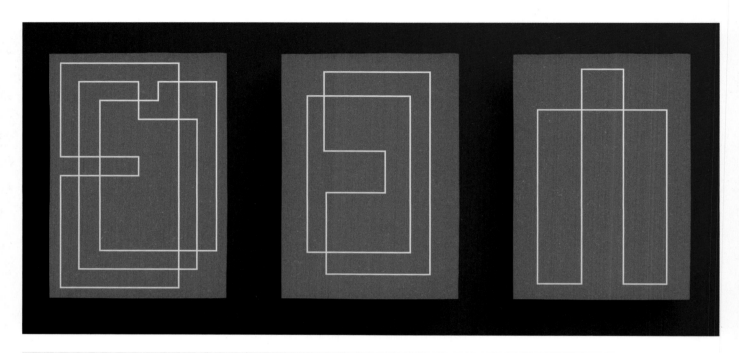

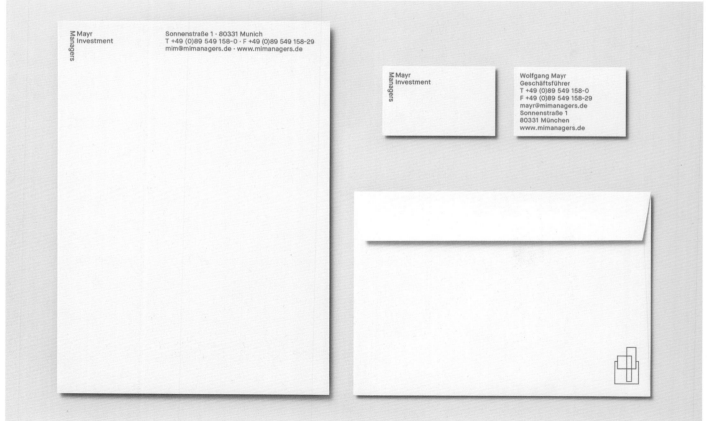

Entwicklung und Anwendung von regelbasierten
estrategien für Investments in Aktien, das ist unsere
Kompetenz und unsere Passion

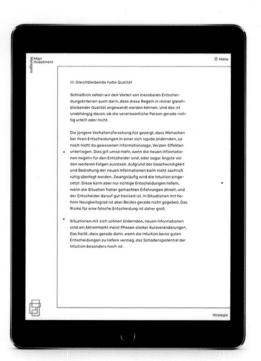

# De Appel Arts Centre

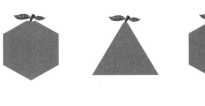

Based on the red apple logo of the brand, the studio developed a new identity where different geometric shapes take the place of the static apple shape in different visual communications, reflecting the essence of the art center.

**Studio: Thonik**

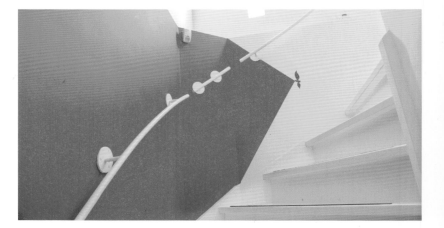

# Phocus

PH[ ]CUS

Phocus is a communication agency with a focus on the pharmaceutical industry and health sector. The identity features a pair of square brackets that represent the letter O and symbolizes the expertise, knowledge and creativity of the brand. This particular symbol has been malleably incorporated into the logo, stationery, catalog, and website layout.

**Designer: Tommaso Taraschi**

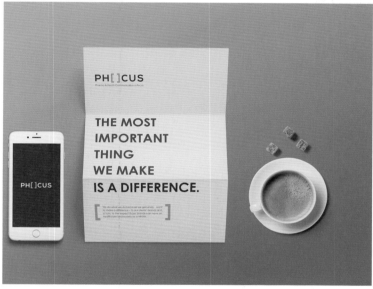

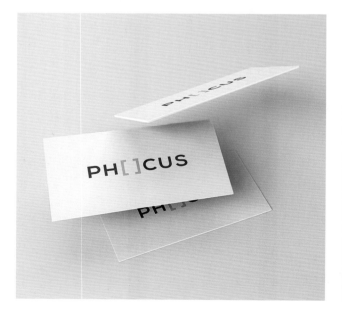

# Teaterbilletter

Teaterbilletter is an online ticket portal, covering more than 100 theatres in Denmark. The new identity was created upon the idea of giving Teaterbilletter a visual language that not only tells about what it sells, but also communicates the magical theatre-going experience. The ticket-symbol was designed to frame different "stories", offering a glimpse of what awaits, while becoming a highly recognizable visual symbol combined with a simple color palette to maintain consistency throughout the identity.

**Studio: IDna Group**
**Designer: Tenna Elisabeth Jacobsen**

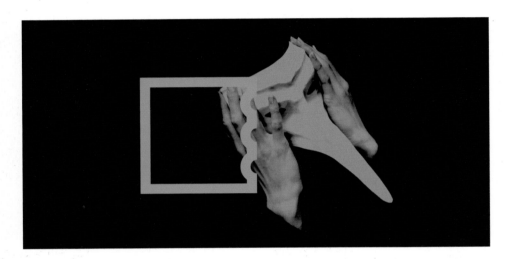

# Nanjing Youth Festival

Nanjing Youth Festival is a global youth festival with the theme of sports, culture and peace. Motivated by the interaction between people and cultures, the identity was intended to invite the young people in Nanjing to elaborate it. They were asked to use black paint to illustrate hand-made symbols that referred to the themes of the festival.

**Studio: Thonik**

# Jazztko II

This poster for a jazz funky show features two triangles that symbolize the two performing DJs. The composition is made of very simple but energetic elements: crossed strokes of yellow paint, wacky vector lines, and bold typography.

**Designer: Krzysztof Iwański**

# Citroën DS Exhibition

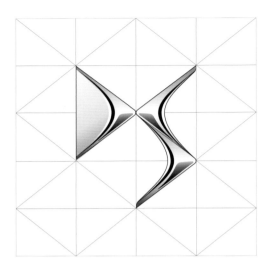

The French auto brand Citroën DS held an exhibition together with industrial designer Jamy Yang in DS shanghai flagship store. Since the exhibition theme was based on the idea of "brand storytelling involved multi-sensorial experience", the designer created a series of graphic symbols by using the grid system of DS's logo, along with shot photos that represent the mystery and uncertainty of human sensorial experience.

**Designer: Wentian Zhang**

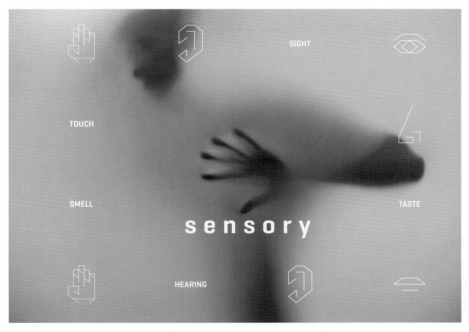

# Isetan Valentine's Day

In the Valentine's Day campaign for the Isetan department store, the letters V and A became color-filled triangles and symbolize boy and the girl respectively, representing a couple that come together and give chocolates. These triangles collectively create a heart shape and other graphics.

**Studio: OUWN**
**Designer: Atsushi Ishiguro, Yumi Idei**

# Assyria—A New Take on Nation

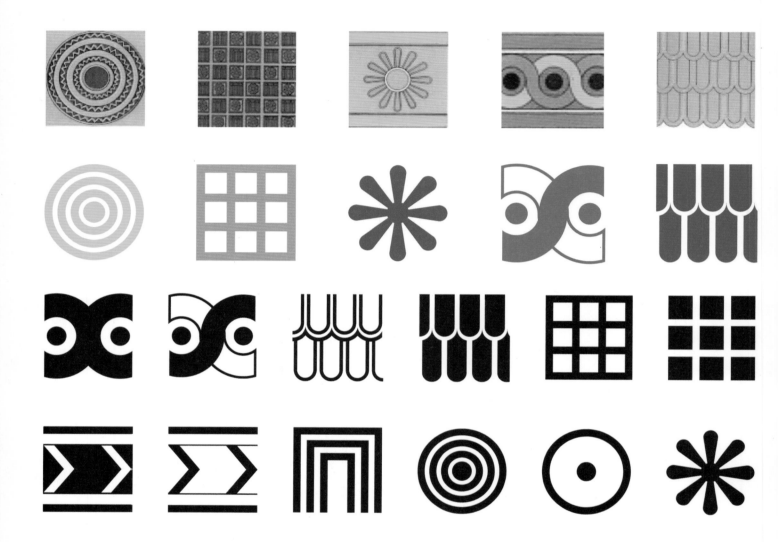

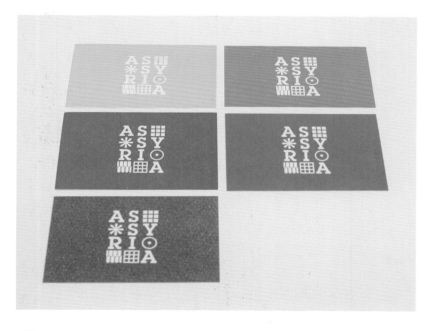

The aim of this project was to create a dynamic visual identity for an unrecognized nation: Assyria. Assyrian culture and tradition and its glorious past have been the starting point of the identity construction. The symbols used in the logo and across the graphics are modern interpretation of Assyrian decorations, representing the many communities within the Assyrian culture that together give life to this nation.

**Designer: Nicolò Fabio Banfi, Anna Borgonovo, Luca Carbone, Clara Citaristi**

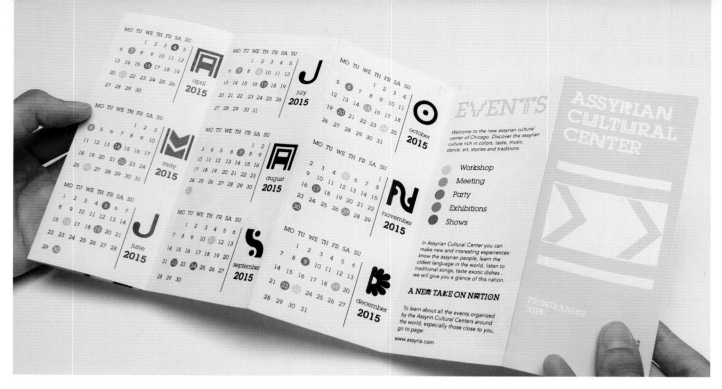

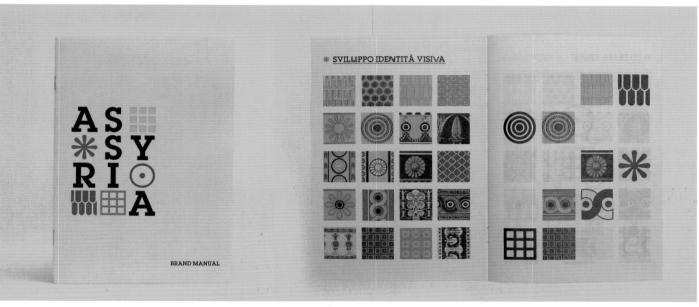

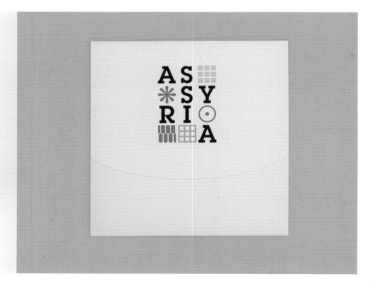

# ADI Awards

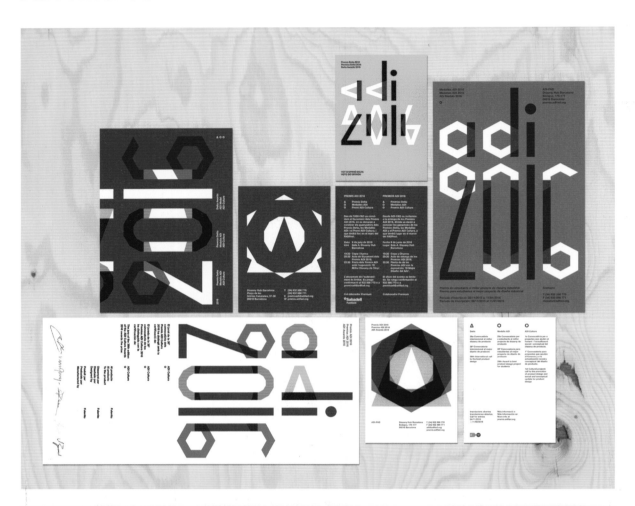

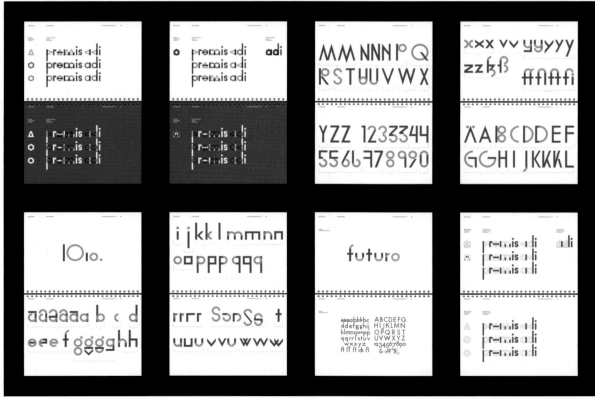

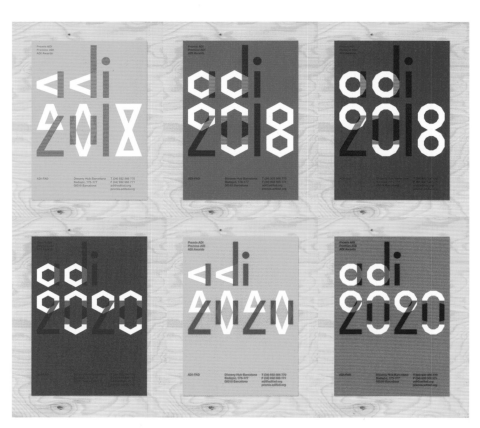

ADI Awards was established by ADI-FAD, a Barcelona based independent organization centered on the dissemination of arts and design. The design team used three symbols—a trigon, a hexagon, and a dodecagon—to characterize different awards. These symbols were further used to build up a striking typography for the main visuals for years to come.

**Studio: TwoPoints.Net**
**Photographer: Carolina Sainz**

# Anne de Grijff

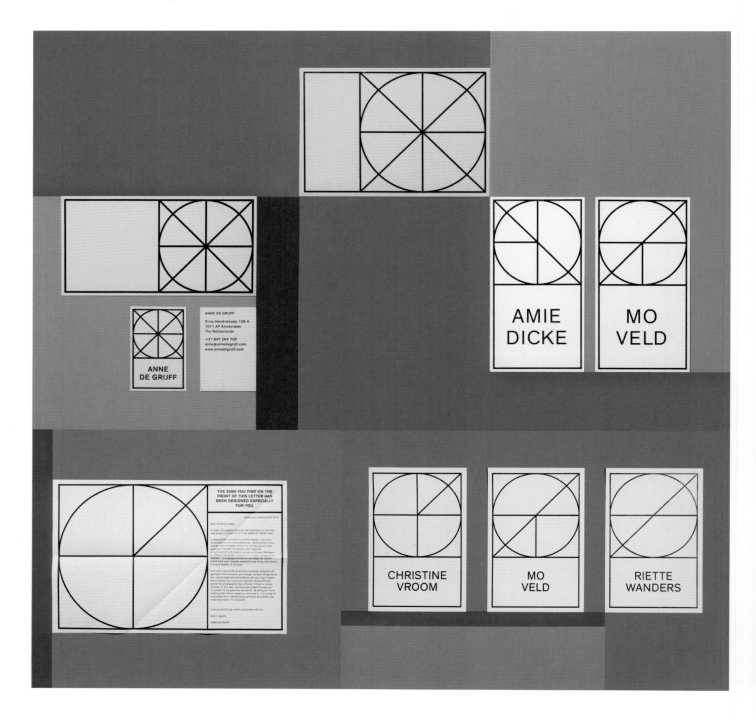

Anne de Grijff is a Dutch fashion designer who focuses on "made to measure", using mainly leather and jerseys, pure wool, luxurious synthetics, and fine silks. To reflect the brand concept and the material palette, a series of flexible grid symbols were made up of square, circle, and cross. The bold framing lines of the graphics can be reconfigured into countless compositions showed up on different design items.

**Studio: Mainstudio**

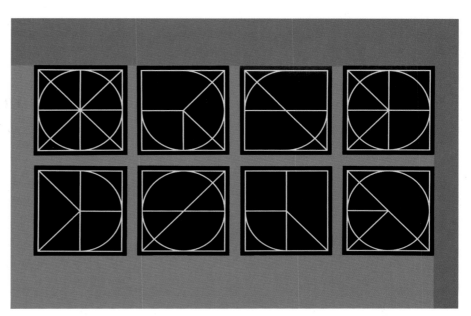

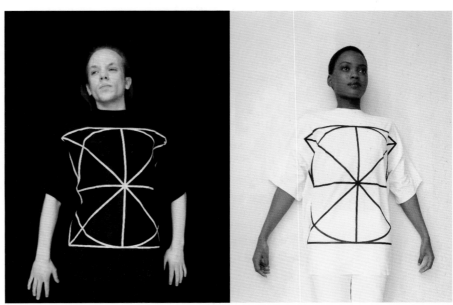

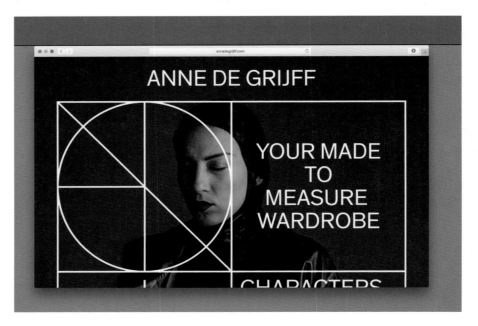

# Edrizzi

Edrizzi is a simple, flexible and most of all eco-friendly system that absorbs paint mist in painting plants. The branding system features a symbol which is derived from the product's functionality and shows the unique filtering technology. This characteristic symbol works as a basis of an extensive visual language including the product categories and its basic form functions as icons for the information graphics.

**Studio: Bruch—Idee&Form**
**Designer: Kurt Glänzer, Josef Heigl**

# Clínica Dr. Carlos Ramos

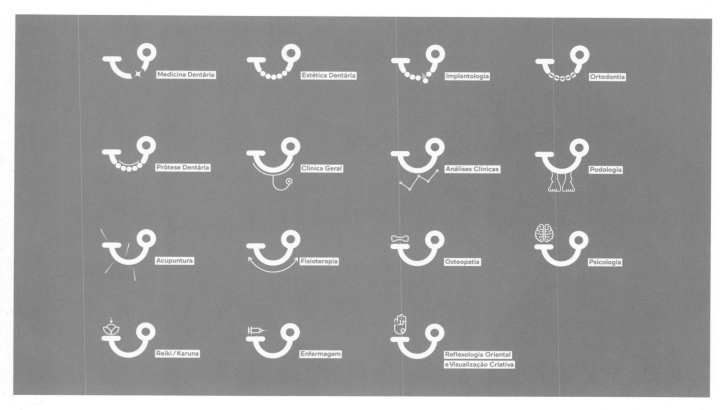

| | | | |
|---|---|---|---|
| Medicina Dentária | Estética Dentária | Implantologia | Ortodontia |
| Prótese Dentária | Clínica Geral | Análises Clínicas | Podologia |
| Acupuntura | Fisioterapia | Osteopatia | Psicologia |
| Reiki / Karuna | Enfermagem | Reflexologia Oriental e Visualização Criativa | |

To create an empathetic and comfortable atmosphere, symbols derived from the logo have been developed with a lighthearted simplicity for different specialties in the clinic so that each service is associated with a smile image.

**Studio: Bullseye**

# Mild Whistle

Mild Whistle's new identity stems from a paradox effect surrounded by a combination of funk layering beyond formality. The identity is enriched though the use of letterpress which brings along the glamour of modernism.

**Studio: Oddds**
**Creative Director: Reinold L., Sarah T.**
**Designer: Sarah T.**

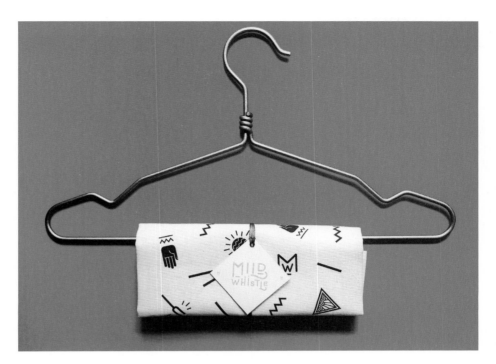

# Útvesztő

| | | | | | |
|---|---|---|---|---|---|

**PÁN**

Az erdei tisztások és legelők szakállas istensége. Szarva, patája és szőrös teste volt. Jellegzetes hangszere a pánsíp.

**HÉPHAISZTOSZ**

A kovácsmesterség, a tűz istene. Ő alkotta Akhilleusz legendás fegyverét és páncélzatát. Héra fia, Aphrodité férje.

**HERMÉSZ**

Az istenek hírnöke, de emellett az utazók védőistene. Kezében kígyós bottal ábrázolták. Zeusz és Maia nimfa gyermeke.

**AKHILLEUSZ**

A harcos őstípusa. Thétisz, a tengeri nimfa és a halandó Peleusz gyermeke. Egyetlen sebezhető pontja a sarka volt.

**KLEIO**

A kilenc múzsa között ő a történetírás és a heroikus költészet megtestesítője. Jelképe a trombita. Zeusz és Mnémoszüné lánya.

**APHRODITÉ**

A szépség és a szerelem istennője. Héphaisztosznak, a kovácsok istenének felesége. Rendkívül szeszélyes és bohó istennő hírében állt.

**ARTEMISZ**

Szűz istennő, aki ezüst íjával és nyilával vadászott, ugyanakkor a vadon oltalmazója. Jupiter és Létó lánya, Apolló ikertestvére.

**ATHENE**

A bölcsesség, az igazságos háború, a művészetek istennője. Jelképei a sisak, a pajzs és a dárda. Zeusz és Métisz gyermeke.

**DIONUSZOSZ**

A bor és a mámor megtestesítője. Jelképei a tirszusz, amely egy bot tobozzal a végén és a borospohár. Zeusz és Szemelé fia.

**ERÓSZ**

A szerelem istene. Egyes források szerint Aphrodité és Árész gyermeke, mások szerint Káosz fia volt. Nyilaival szerelmet keltett vagy oltott ki.

**KRONOSZ**

Uranosz és Gaia gyermeke, a tizenkét titán leghatalmabja. Az olümposzi istenek atyja. Nevének jelentése idő.

**ÁRÉSZ**

A háború istene. A harc pusztító erejét, az őrjöngő küzdelmet és a férfias erőt testesítette meg. Zeusz és Héra gyermeke.

**HEKATÉ**

A varázslás, a sötétség és az éjszaka istennője, illetve az egyik holdistenség. Három testtel, arccal vagy három pár karral jeleníthető meg.

**HÉRA**

Zeusz testvére és felesége, az olümposzi istenek úrnője. A házasságot és a születést védelmező istennő. Egyik jelképe a páva, amely szekerét húzta.

**HÉRAKLÉSZ**

Zeusz és Alkméné félisten gyermeke. Kiállta a 12 próbát, amely kitartásáról és harciasságáról tanúskodott.

**IKAROSZ**

A lázadás, a szófogadatlanság, a kíváncsiság megtestesítője. Daidalosz fia.

**TÜKHÉ**

A sors, a végzet istennője. Bekötött szemmel ábrázolták, mellette egy kerék, az állandó változás jelképe. Ókeanosz és Téthüsz leánya.

**GRÁCIÁK**

A szépséget és a bájt megtestesítő három Grácia, más néven Khariszok, Aphrodité hírnökei voltak. Zeusz és Eurünomé lányai.

**MEGAIRA**

Az Erinnüszöknek, a véres bosszúállás istennőinek egyike. Kígyóhajuk, kutyafejük és denevér szárnyuk volt. Gaia és Uranosz gyermekei.

**PERSZEPHONÉ**

Hádész elrabolta, így lett az alvilág királynője. Sorsa eldőlt, amikor a gránátalmából evett. Démétér és Zeusz lánya.

**POSZEIDON**

A folyók, tavak, tengerek istene. Ő szelidített elsőként lovakat. Jelképe a háromágú szigony. Kronosz és Rheia fia.

**SZELÉNÉ**

A Hold megszemélyesítője, Hüperión és Theia titánok gyermeke. Fején fekvő félholddal ábrázolták, szekerét fehér lovak húzták.

**ZEUSZ**

Az istenek és a mindenség királya, az ég és a villámok ura. Hírnöke a sas, megnyilatkozása a villámlás. Kronosz fia.

**HÁDÉSZ**

Az alvilág istene, a holtak ura. Birodalmának kapuját három fejű kutyája, Kerberosz őrizte. Kronosz és Rheia gyermeke.

Útvesztő game is a redesigned and further developed form of Bolondos labirintus (Playful Labyrinth), an existing board game available in shops. The biggest changes are the theme and the visuals, which is now connected to the Greek mythology. The aim of the game is to create walkable paths by moving the labyrinth around and to get to as many mythological figures as possible.

**Designer: Luca Héjja**

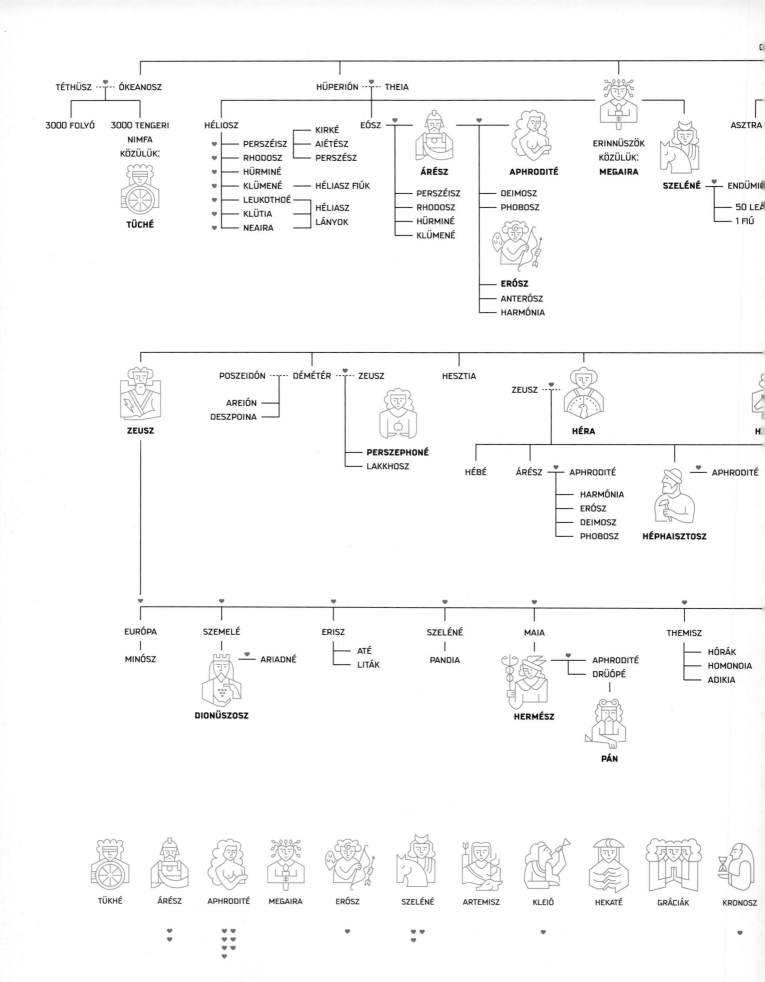

TÉTHÜSZ ····· ÓKEANOSZ

3000 FOLYÓ    3000 TENGERI
              NIMFA
              KÖZÜLÜK:

**TÜCHÉ**

HÜPERIÓN ····· THEIA

HÉLIOSZ

- PERSZÉISZ — KIRKÉ
- RHODOSZ — AIÉTÉSZ
- HÜRMINÉ — PERSZÉSZ
- KLÜMENÉ — HÉLIASZ FIÚK
- LEUKOTHOÉ
- KLÜTIA — HÉLIASZ
- NEAIRA — LÁNYOK

EÓSZ

**ÁRÉSZ**

- PERSZÉISZ
- RHODOSZ
- HÜRMINÉ
- KLÜMENÉ

**APHRODITÉ**

- DEIMOSZ
- PHOBOSZ

**ERÓSZ**
- ANTERÓSZ
- HARMÓNIA

ERINNÜSZÖK
KÖZÜLÜK:
**MEGAIRA**

**SZELÉNÉ** ····· ENDÜMIO

- 50 LEÁ
- 1 FIÚ

ASZTRA

**ZEUSZ**

POSZEIDÓN ····· DÉMÉTÉR ····· ZEUSZ

- AREIÓN
- DESZPOINA

**PERSZEPHONÉ**
- LAKKHOSZ

HESZTIA

ZEUSZ ····· **HÉRA**

- HÉBÉ
- ÁRÉSZ ····· APHRODITÉ
  - HARMÓNIA
  - ERÓSZ
  - DEIMOSZ
  - PHOBOSZ

**HÉPHAISZTOSZ** ····· APHRODITÉ

H.

EURÓPA

MINÓSZ

SZEMELÉ

**DIONÜSZOSZ** ····· ARIADNÉ

ERISZ

- ATÉ
- LITÁK

SZELÉNÉ

PANDIA

MAIA

**HERMÉSZ** ····· APHRODITÉ
- DRÜÓPÉ

**PÁN**

THEMISZ

- HÓRÁK
- HOMONOIA
- ADIKIA

TÜKHÉ    ÁRÉSZ    APHRODITÉ    MEGAIRA    ERÓSZ    SZELÉNÉ    ARTEMISZ    KLEIÓ    HEKATÉ    GRÁCIÁK    KRONOSZ

OSZ

EURÜBIA — IAPETOSZ — KLÜMENÉ

ASZ — SZTÜX — PERSZÉSZ

KOIOSZ ---- PHOIBÉ

RHEIA

ATLASZ — PLÉIÓNÉ — HÜÁSZOK
PLEIÁSZOK

MENOITOSZ
PROMÉTHEUSZ — PANDÓRA
EPIMÉTHEUSZ — PANDÓRA

BIÉ
NIKÉ
KRATOSZ
ZÉLOSZ

LÉTÓ — ZEUSZ

ASZTERIA — PERSZÉSZ

KRONOSZ

PROPHASZISZ
METAMELEIA
PÜRRHA

APOLLÓN

♥ DAPHNÉ
♥ KÜRÉNÉ
♥ HEKABÉ
♥ KASSZANDRA
♥ KORÓNISZ
♥ ISZKÜSZ
♥ HÜAKINTHOSZ
♥ KÜPARISSZOSZ

**ARTEMISZ**

**HEKATÉ**

AMPHITRITÉ — 

**POSZEIDÓN**

PÉGASZOSZ
KHRÜSZAÓR
PRÓTEUSZ
POLÜPHÉMOSZ
AREIÓN
DESZPOINA

♥ MEDUSZA
♥ NAIDA
♥ THOÓSZA
♥ DÉMÉTÉR

TRITÓN — NÉREISZEK
KÖZÜLÜK:
THETISZ — PÉLEUSZ

RHODÉ — HÉLIOSZ

BENTHESZIKÜMÉ

KÜMOPOLEIA — BRIAREÓSZ

**AKHILLEUSZ**

♥ DIÓNÉ ÓKEÁNUSZ
APHRODITÉ

♥ MNÉMOSZÜNÉ

♥ ÉLEKTRA PLEIÁSZ
IASZIÓN

♥ EURÜNOMÉ ÓKEÁNUSZ

♥ DÉMÉTÉR
PERSZEPHONÉ
LAKKHOSZ

♥ ALKMÉNÉ — HELÉNÉ

MÚZSÁK
KÖZÜLÜK:
**KLEIÓ**

KHARISZOK
MÁS NÉVEN:
**GRÁCIÁK**

**HERAKLÉSZ**

DIONÜSZOSZ    ZEUSZ    PERSZEPHONÉ    HERMÉSZ    HÉRA    HÉPHAISZTOSZ    HÁDÉSZ    HERAKLÉSZ    POSZEIDÓN    AKHILLEUSZ    PÁN

♥ ♥
♥ ♥ ♥ ♥ ♥
♥ ♥ ♥ ♥ ♥
♥ ♥ ♥ ♥ ♥
♥ ♥ ♥ ♥ ♥
♥ ♥ ♥ ♥ ♥
♥ ♥ ♥ ♥
♥ ♥
♥ ♥
♥
♥
♥ ♥
♥ ♥
♥ ♥
♥ ♥ ♥
♥
♥ ♥
♥

# Ethan Lee Photography

Dark tone was given to the business card for the sense of tranquility emitted by the photography works of Ethan Lee. On the front side of the card is a representative work of Lee which sets up the visual context, while the abstract shapes of viewfinder, light and shutter in silver foil floating throughout the design intensify the visual emotion.

**Designer: Sion Hsu**

# Wild Exile Image

Wild Exile Image is a documentary photography team recording local customs across China. Ink was used as a symbol of the oriental culture, hot-stamped squares as a symbol of the recorded images, and dots as a symbol of moments.

**Designer: Sion Hsu**
**Photographer: Ben Cen**

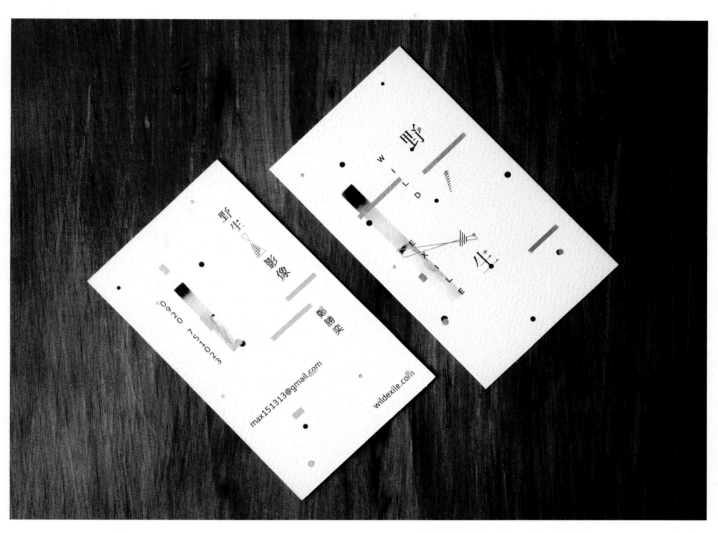

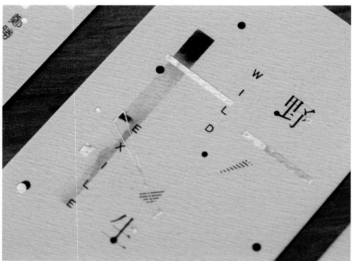

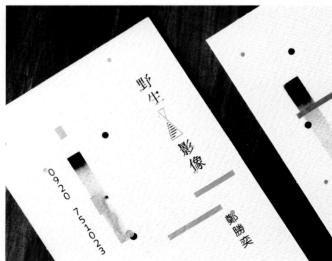

# T.Rex Music Studio

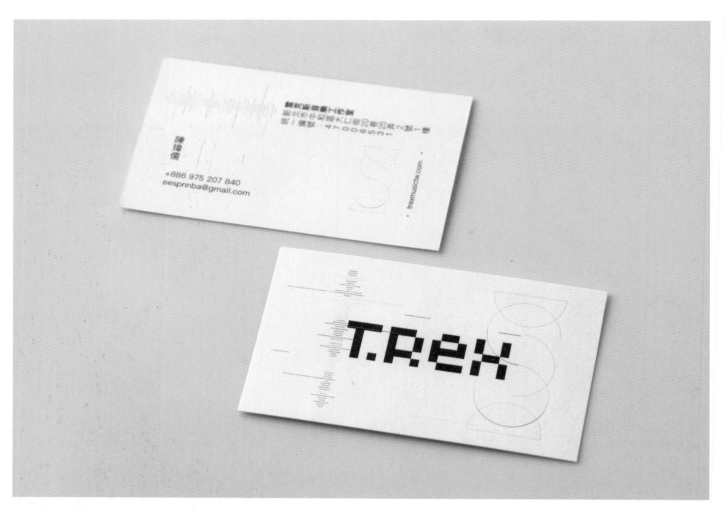

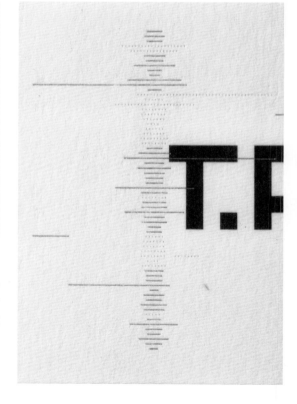

In this business card design for a musical team, dots were used as a symbol of the digital world. A work of asymmetry and balance was formed with the dots placed in the smallest distance, complemented by golden waves that symbolize melodies.

**Designer: Sion Hsu**

# Éire Stamps

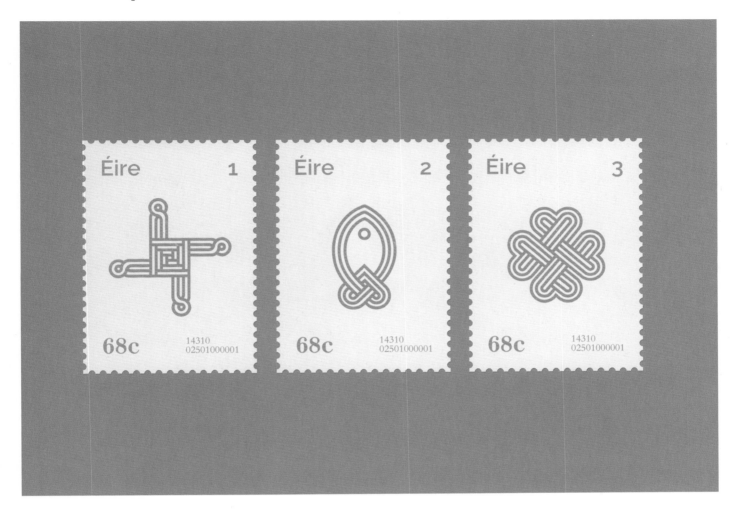

The stamps feature three particular symbols in the Celtic style of weaving which has been in use for thousands of years and has its origins in the artwork of the Roman Empire. The stroke weight of the symbols is identical to the spacing between the lines: this allows the stamps to be substantially varied but maintain their places in the series.

**Designer: Aaron Canning**

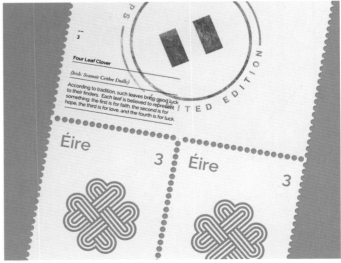

# D&R

The idea for this wedding invitation design was to create two fields of emotions with small graphic elements floating from one side to another as a wave of happiness. These elements are in primary shapes, opposite but complementary to each other.

**Designer: Marta Veludo**

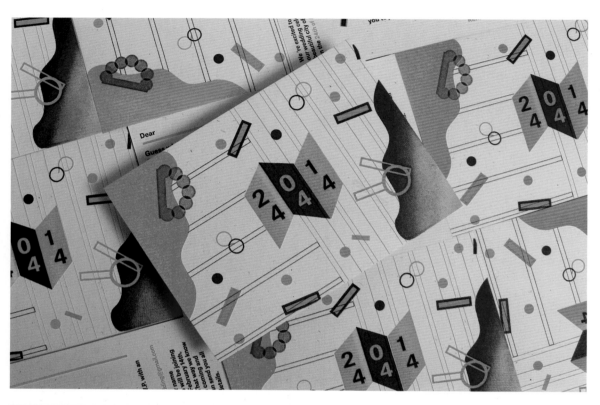

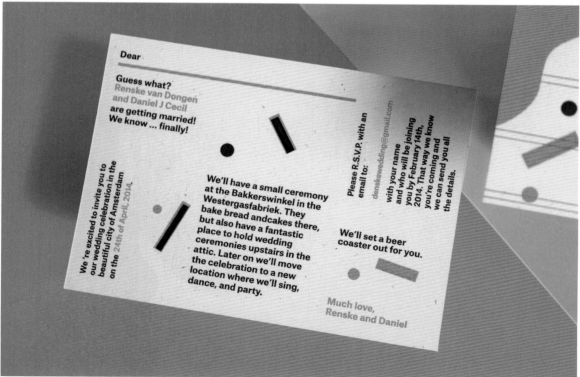

# Kunstmarket

Different symbols have been created in the graphic kit to represent each creative activity included in the Kunstmarket (Art Market). The handmade feeling alludes to the medium used by most participating artists.

**Designer: Marta Veludo, Sue Doeksen**

# Minim Playing Cards

Minim is a deck of playing cards that dallies with the idea of how much one can take away while still maintaining a playable deck. The minimalistic geometric symbols are reductive versions of hearts, clubs, diamonds, and spades, and a simple diagonal line marks the back of the cards.

**Designer: Joe Doucet**

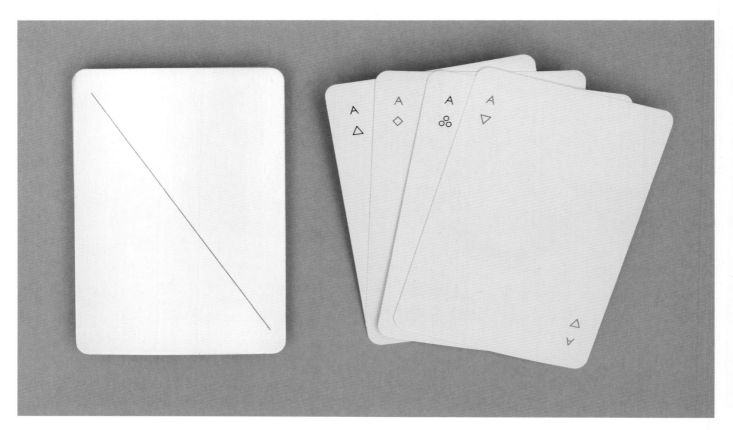

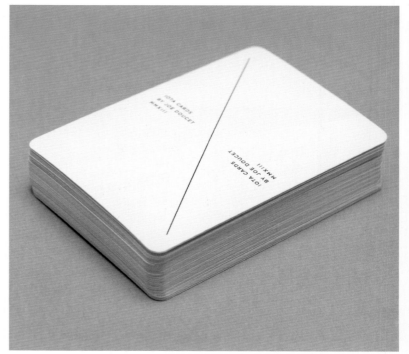

# Morishita Music School

Taking inspiration from the German folk song "Ich bin ein Musikant" which is familiarly known as "Animal Musicians of Forest" in Japan, the designer created symbols of animals playing music. It vividly reflects the school's teaching method of using various musical instruments and body movements.

**Studio: tegusu Inc.**
**Designer: Masaomi Fujita**

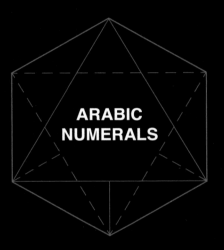

ARABIC
NUMERALS

# Brahmi Numerals

| – | = | ≡ | + | Һ | φ | ? | ৮ | ? |
|---|---|---|---|---|---|---|---|---|
| 1 | 2 | 3 | 4 | 5 | 6 | 7 | 8 | 9 |

# Eastern Arabic Numerals

| ١ | ٢ | ٣ | ٤ | ٥ | ٦ | ٧ | ٨ | ٩ | ٠ |
|---|---|---|---|---|---|---|---|---|---|
| 1 | 2 | 3 | 4 | 5 | 6 | 7 | 8 | 9 | 0 |

# Indian Numerals

| १ | २ | ३ | ४ | ५ | ६ | ७ | ८ | ९ | ० |
|---|---|---|---|---|---|---|---|---|---|
| 1 | 2 | 3 | 4 | 5 | 6 | 7 | 8 | 9 | 0 |

# Modern Arabic Numerals

1 2 3 4 5 6 7 8 9 0

The invention of numerical symbols marks a big step forward in human being's intellectual development.

Arabic numerals, also known as Hindu-Arabic numerals, are at present the numerical symbols most commonly used across the world, with only ten digits: 1, 2, 3, 4, 5, 6, 7, 8, 9 and 0. This particular numeration system became widely adopted thanks to its easily recognized shapes and efficient algorithm.

It is believed that Arabic numerals' predecessor is Brahmi numerals, an ancient non-place-value system in the 3rd century B.C. India. Indians developed the prototype of modern Arabic numerals and computation, and later a dot symbol for the concept of zero, which is crucial in the formation of decimal place-value system. From the inscriptions at a temple in Gwalior, India, we learn that in the 9th century a small circle had been used to represent zero. As the Arab Empire expanded its territory to as far as India, the Arabs got acquainted with the Indian computation system and adopted it. The Arabs then spread the Hindu-Arabic numerals to Europe where they evolved to be the modern Arabic numerals. Particularly from the 15th century when the printing was introduced, the symbols for these numerals became standardized. There is also some evidence that the modern Arabic numerals took their graphic forms and algorithm system from Arabic alphabet and writing fashion. Nowadays, instead of the modern ones, some Arabic countries use Eastern Arabic numerals, which were developed based on the old numerals brought from India. Although the origin of the numerals' forms remains uncertain, it is true that the modern Arabic numerals have undergone a long and complicated transformation journey during which different cultures had been involved.

Today there are slightly different ways of reproducing the Arabic numerals in different parts of the world and infinite ways of presenting them in graphic design world.

# Adidas Gym

Adidas is one of the world's leading producers of sporting goods. The interior design of Adidas fitness center in Herzogenaurach communicates the enterprise's spirit. Inspired by the colorful world of sports and the jersey number, the design team employed different colors and digits in the wall graphics, furniture, and lighting.

Some of the numbers on the wall indicate the milestones of sports and of Adidas history, for example 1949 the foundation of the brand, 1954 the Miracle of Bern. The graphics of each room echo a different sport and atmosphere.

**Designer: ZieglerBürg Büro für Gestaltung**
**Communication Design: Büro Uebele**
**Photographer: Brigida González**

# 7-Eleven Coffee

To change the customer perception of 7-Eleven coffee towards a more modern and urban one, the choices of colors, materials and details were made to balance a quick buying process with a comfortable coffee break. Cups and packaging were redesigned where the iconic stripes have been used as the starting point for playful and bold treatments of each identity carrier.

**Studio: BVD**

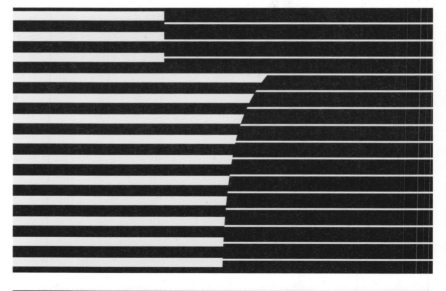

# Olympic Games Oslo 2022

OSLO2O22
Applicant City

OSLO2O22
Applicant City

The visual identity for Oslo 2022's Applicant City bid honors the inherent simplicity and openness of Nordic culture. The circular forms of the letter O and the number 0, as well as the repetition of forms in the letter S and the number 2 lend themselves to a graphic element constructed out of just a few geometrical shapes. Combined with colors inspired by the Olympic rings, the result forms the basis for the identity in balance of playfulness and strictness.

**Studio: Snøhetta**
**Photographer: Johan Wildhagen**

# Teatros Luchana Madrid

The identity plays with the idea of the theater's division into four spaces and the different types of show in each one. The spaces are represented by numbers 1, 2, 3, and 4, each in a different typeface as a metaphor of different characteristics.

**Studio: Toormix**
**Photographer: Matt Lazenby, Vaca Estudio, Toormix**

# Nineteen—LSAD Fashion Show

This is a visual identity for LSAD Fashion Department's Fashion Show. The title Nineteen referred to the 19 designers participating in the show. The focus was on presenting these 19 individuals with dark and ambiguous visuals. Therefore, a modern visual juxtaposition was made, combining a mix of typographic elements with intriguing visuals.

**Designer: Brett O'Mahony, Louise O'Doherty, Magdalena Schiller-Sæther**

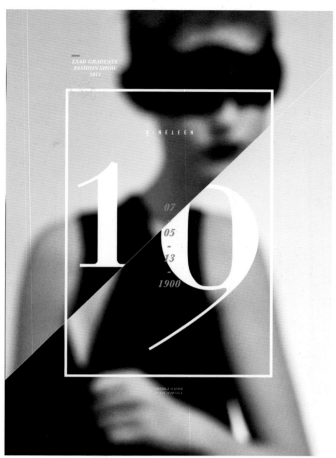

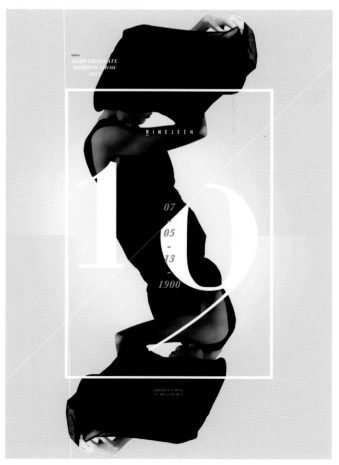

# Lettera 22

Created on the 15th anniversary of the Italian industrialist Adriano Olivetti's death, the project is a packaging for a DVD collection about architecture, arts and design. The graphic highlights a monogram composition of "22" in a minimal but lively style. Playing with the number 22, the designers arrived at the idea of the black inked ribbon of the Olivetti Lettera 22 typewriter.

**Studio: Artiva Design**
**Designer: Daniele De Batté, Davide Sossi**

# Year Round Calendar

The eight rolls of 10 meters tape allow all possibilities of time panning and organizing, in a way that leaves the finishing touch to the consumer and creates a DIY feeling. The clear, uncomplicated aesthetics and the use of the classic lettertype Helvetica form the basis for an enjoyable and timeless design.

**Studio: mo man tai**
**Designer: Ulrike Jurklies**

# Best of Nature

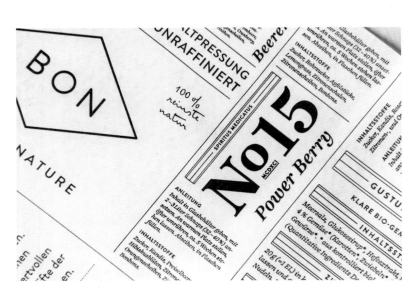

Nature refrains from the unnecessary. So does the new brand identity for Best of Nature natural product. Colors, shapes, and numerical system act as organizing tools and add clarity within the product range, maintaining the focus on the products and the finest essence of nature.

**Studio: moodley brand identity**
**Photographer: Michael Königshofer**

# Mercado 1143

Mercado 1143 is a gourmet store with a tasting zone dedicated to the promotion of 100% Portuguese products from local producers. The number 1143 is the year of the foundation of Portugal, developed from the imagination of a post code for this country. It is a coat of arms as well as a timeless seal of warranty.

**Studio: Mola Ativism**
**Designer: Rui Morais**
**Photographer: Nuno Correia**

# Just T

The tea packaging features a typography concept where the numbers from 0 to 24 were assigned to each variety by being made up of the blend inside.

**Designer: Christian von der Heide**
**Photographer: Inhouse**

# GreenLife Tea

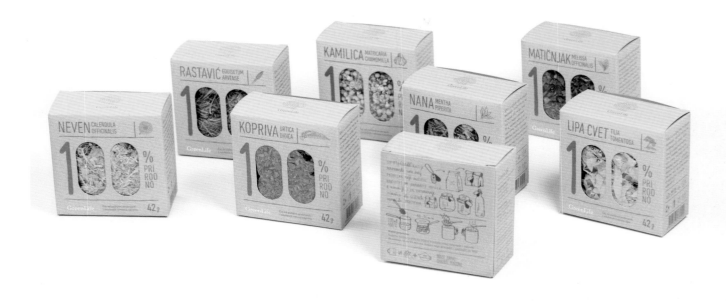

The brief of this redesigned packaging is practicality in terms of packaging process and transportation. The transparent double zero on the front of the packaging discloses the tea inside and emphasizes the "100%" at the same time. The tags with a rubber band that comes with the box are in fact the opening of the double zero, used to fasten the plastic bag or other food containers.

**Studio: Bullsheep**
**Designer: Filip Nemet**
**Photographer: Pavle Taboroši**

# Sans
# & Sans Atelier

Tea bags design for Sans & Sans.

**Studio: Requena**
**Designer: Andrés Requena**
**Photographer: Koldo Castillo**

# Back to Basics

Back to Basics is a self-promotion kit which aims to evoke the basics of creation: light, paper and colors. The kit consists of 6 packages, each one printed with a number indicating the opening sequence and a content-related phrase.

**Designer: Sofía Maltos Martínez**

# La Vinya del Vuit

La Vinya del Vuit is a limited production wine produced by a collective of eight fellow winemakers. The word "vuit" in Catalan language means "eight". The identity of this product is being renewed on an annual basis to build a particular and diverse collection. Through a poetic interpretation with a sensorial blast and the mix of vibrant colors opposed to the serious visual tradition, a bright symbol of the number 8 blooms to tell a story about the year's harvest.

**Studio: JJ Bertran Studio**
**Designer: Joan Josep Bertran**

# John & John Crisps

Each variety of John & John crisps is easily distinguished through the packaging by the engraved images, numbers, and individual color codes from the nautical flag alphabet.

**Studio: Peter Schmidt Group**
**Designer: Katrin Niesen**

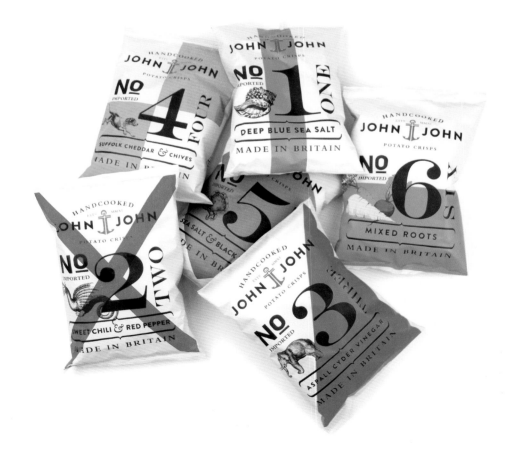

# Wayfinding for Innovation Center

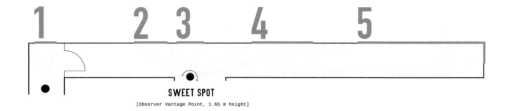

**SWEET SPOT**
[Observer Vantage Point, 1.65 m height]

LAB [1 - 3]
GAB [1 - 3]

LAB [4 - 5]
GAB [4 - 6]

COZINHA
PLAYGROUND

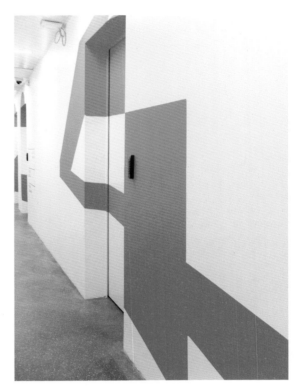

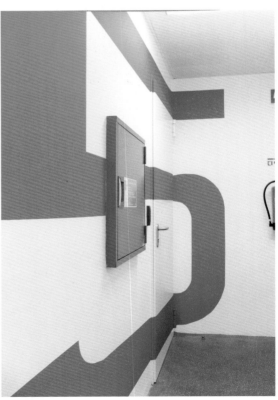

By using an anamorphic typography process, the studio established a connection between simple numbers and scientific measurements and challenged the conventional idea that innovation can only be realized in high technology. As the five entrances to the laboratories are aligned on the same wall, the numbers are visualized in perfect shape and size from the sweet spot before the number 3. The corridors have become full of color and life—science and research are all about creativity and discoveries.

**Studio: Claan**
**Designer: Clara Vieira, Andreas Eberharter**

# Tegusu Calendar

This is a self-promotional calendar, featuring the designer's original number fonts made of simple geometric shapes and vivid colors.

**Studio: tegusu Inc.**
**Designer: Masaomi Fujita**

# A.P.J. Calendars

Designed for Art Print Japan, this calendar plays with an infinite amount of styles and ways of expression though typography. The project well embodies the studio's signature aesthetics, which is to recreate the timeless elements in a contemporary way and let the essential shine through simplicity.

**Studio: Homework**

homework

CALENDAR 2013

# Everyday Graphic Calendar

With the hope to reintroduce daily calendar which was used by earlier generations and is occasionally seen these days, the studio designed a different graphic for each day of the year. For national holidays and some anniversaries the graphics were embedded with corresponding meanings, while the rest offered an opportunity for wild imagination.

**Studio: Ordinary People**

194

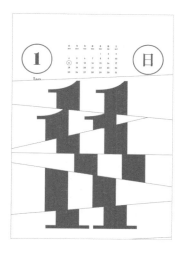   

 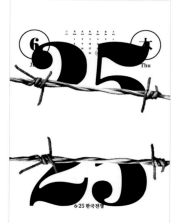  

# Graphic Designer's Portfolio

This is the designer's personal portfolio designed in a simple and clean style. The numbers representing different work disciplines are particularly eye-catching, inviting viewers to open the portfolio for further contents.

**Designer: Hermes Mazali**

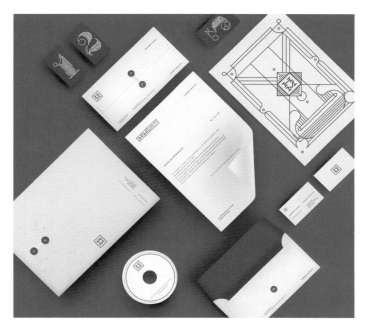

# Village Taipei
# Annual Brochure

URS (Urban Regeneration Station) is a platform, a network and a campaign initiated by the Urban Redevelopment Office of Taipei City Government. The space can be used as a public space for social interaction, a venue for exhibitions and a location for experimental actions. Each URS is named by its house number, which has been the inspiration and basis for the brochure design for each number has its own voice and characters.

**Studio: Onion Design Associates**
**Art Director: Andrew Wong**
**Designer: Charly Chen**

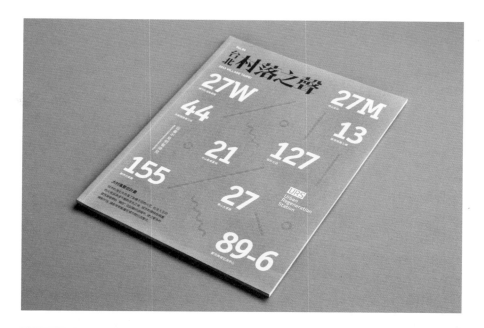

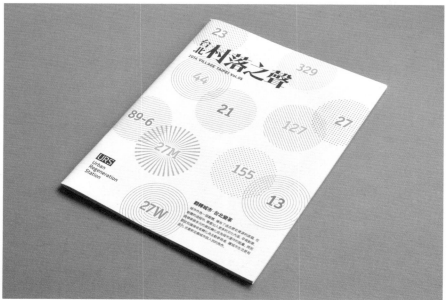

# Letterpress Calendar

The calendar comes with three different covers, featuring remarks about design and designers. It is also an experiment of typography with the numbers to push the visual possibilities offered by the letterpress printing process. Each month number has been uniquely designed, embedded with the designer's passion for old numbers, papers and ornaments.

**Studio: Mr Cup**
**Designer: Fabien Barral**

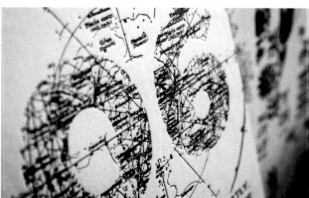

# Shanghai Ranking

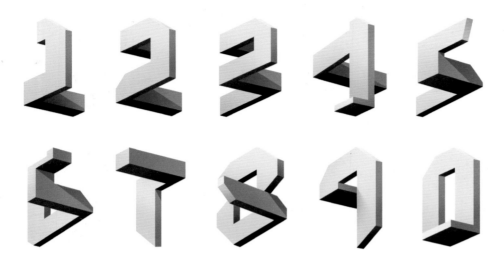

The numbers were developed as part of the *Shanghai Jiao Tong Top 200 Research Universities* book design. The idea is based on ribbons and medals awarded for excellence within a field, echoing the subject matter of the book.

**Studio: Sawdust**
**Designer: Rob Gonzalez, Jonathan Quainton**

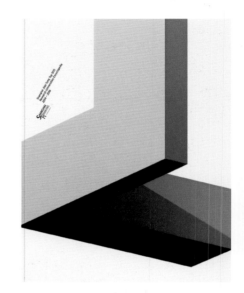

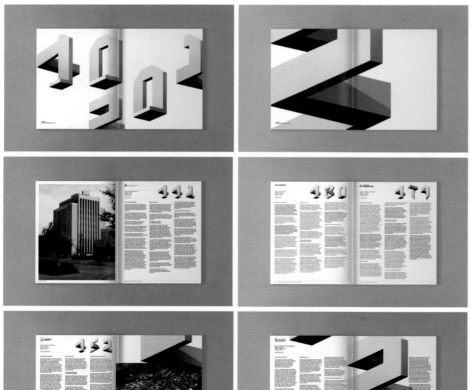

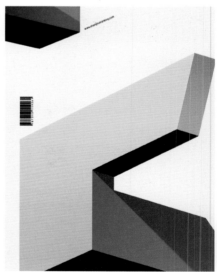

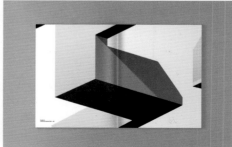

# Fundació Miró 40 Years

The visual identity for the 40th anniversary campaign of the cultural center Fundació Miró was designed under two main objectives: to generate a highly recognizable iconic symbol, and to relate the center with the people of Barcelona through relevant dates of the last 40 years. The answer was a number 40 inspired by the outlines of the center building, and a typographical system based on which the key dates of the campaign were composed.

**Studio: Mucho**
**Designer: Marc Català**
**Photographer: Borja Ballbé**

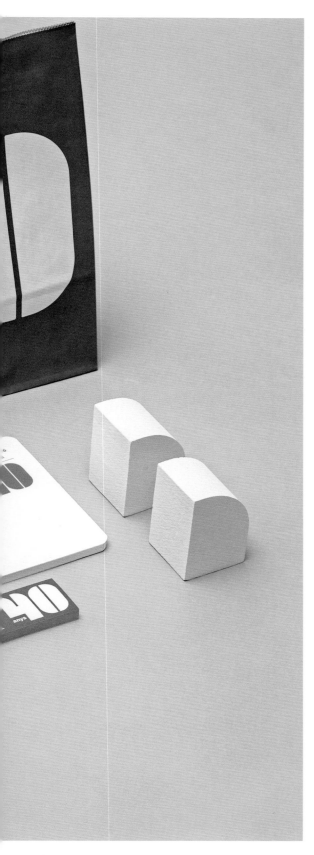

The overall idea of this project was to illustrate different important days in a person's life and how they affect one's financial situation. Based upon the selected dates and the related stories, the designer brought the numbers to life through handcrafts and made the visuals distinctive yet cohesive.

**Studio: Reklamebureauet OS**
**Creative Director: Jabali Ravn**
**Designer: Yulia Brodskaya**
**Photographer: Michael Leznik**

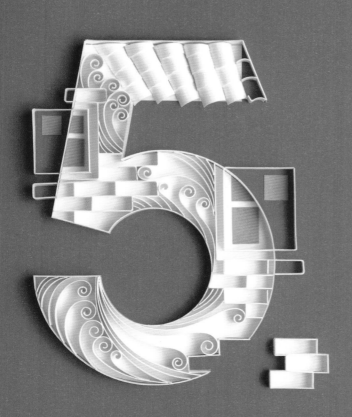

# We Love Geometry

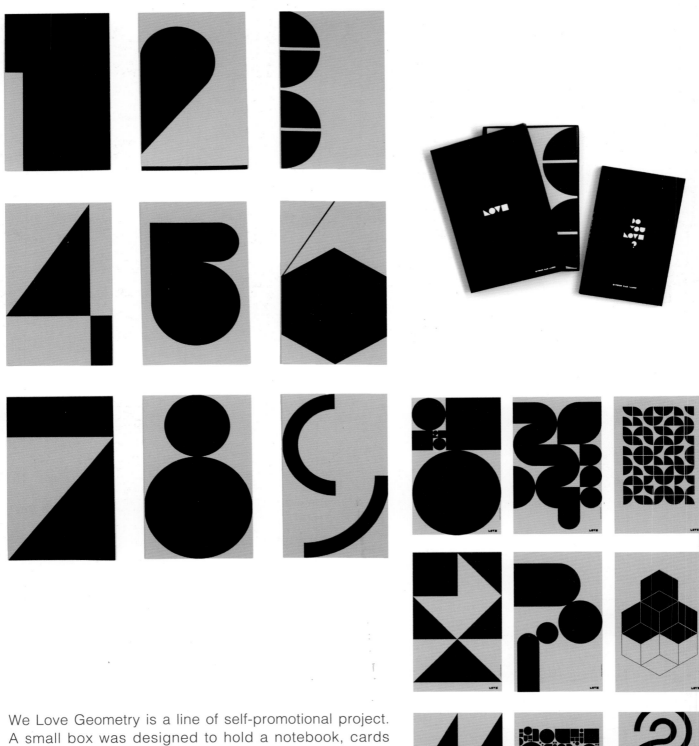

We Love Geometry is a line of self-promotional project. A small box was designed to hold a notebook, cards and fold-out posters. On the back of each card are some very basic notes on geometry based on which the corresponding poster is subtly related in shape and structure. Card number 3 refers to the modular grid, number 7 the triangle, number 9 the line, and so on.

**Designer: Ibán Ramón Rodríguez**

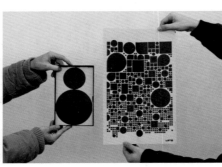

# Duintjer Signage

The signage for building Duintjer in Amsterdam features floor numbers that are constructed out of lines as a reference to the modular character of the building. The outer shape of the numerals is based on the contours of a clear sans serif typeface, while the lines of the numerals are moving in different directions to create 3D visuals.

**Studio: OK200**
**Designer: Mattijs de Wit, Koen Knevel**

# Droom Van Helderheid

Droom Van Helderheid introduces the visual identity development in the Netherlands from 1960 to 1975. The book designer made use of the simplicity and protruding characteristics of the Arabic numerals to gain attention and underline the keyword of the theme.

**Designer: Wang Zhi-Hong**

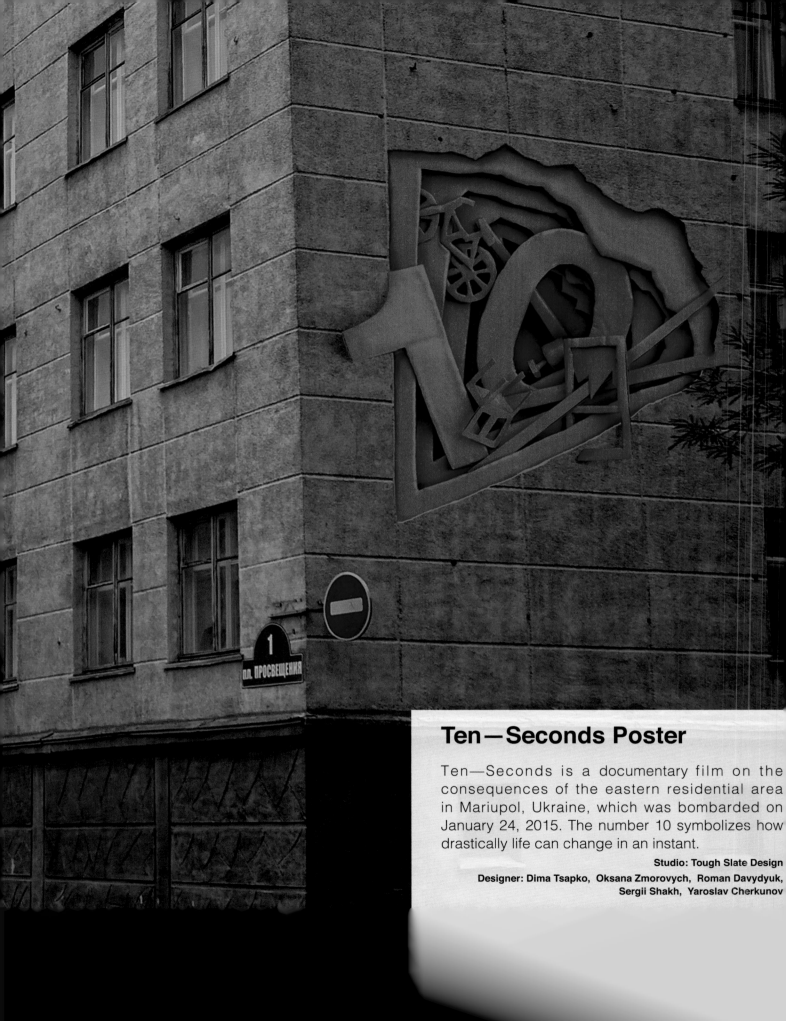

## Ten—Seconds Poster

Ten—Seconds is a documentary film on the consequences of the eastern residential area in Mariupol, Ukraine, which was bombarded on January 24, 2015. The number 10 symbolizes how drastically life can change in an instant.

**Studio: Tough Slate Design**
**Designer: Dima Tsapko, Oksana Zmorovych, Roman Davydyuk, Sergii Shakh, Yaroslav Cherkunov**

Ten—Seconds

A—DOCUMENTARY—FILM
OF—MARIUPOL—BOMBING
FEB—2015

#BABYLON'13

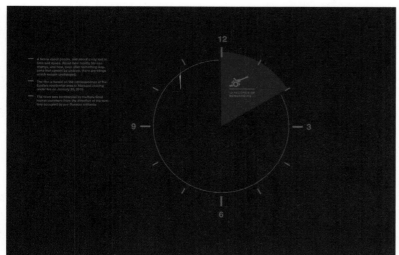

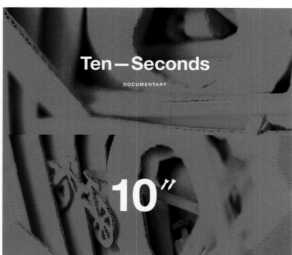

Ten—Seconds

DOCUMENTARY

10″

10″

# Yapa

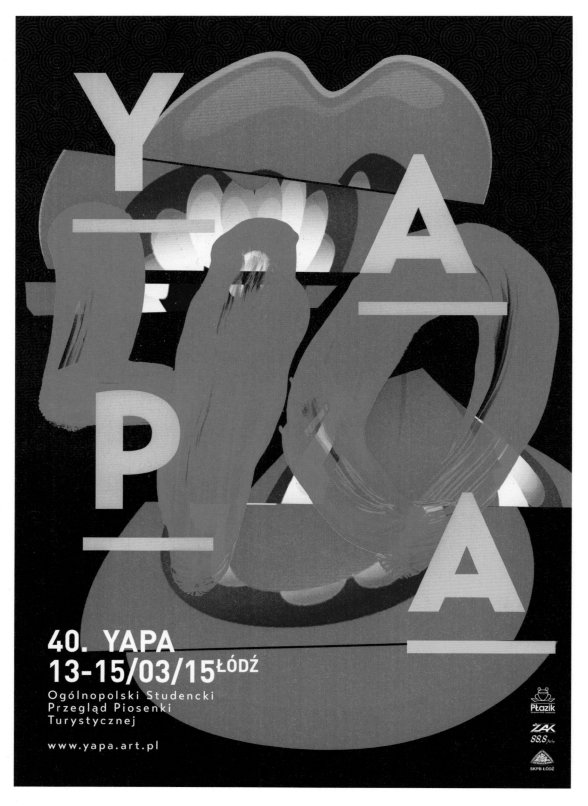

Yapa is a songwriter festival in Lodz, Poland. Yapa means loudmouth, so the poster adopted an illustration of a mouth as the background and emphasized the bold and strong typography.

**Designer: Krzysztof Iwanski**

# Znak

This cover designed for the 70th anniversary of the magazine underlines the title —"does religion have a future?"—with the artistic numeral printed with gold foil.

**Designer: Krzysztof Iwanski**

# Posters for I DO

The project I DO is a series of architectural discussions presented by startup or famous architectural studios. The posters blended the pictures provided by those studios and the appointed dates of discussions—10th April, 24th May, etc.

**Creative Director: Alexander Vasin**
**Designer: Alexander Vasin, Sveta Kuzmicheva**

ДИСКУССИЯ #3
ПРОЕКТНАЯ ГРУППА ВОСЕМЬ / 8 —— СЕРГЕЙ СИТАР
17 АПРЕЛЯ В 19:00
АРХИТЕКТУРНАЯ ШКОЛА МАРШ, ARTPLAY

ДИСКУССИЯ #6
АРХИТЕКТУРНАЯ СТУДИЯ ПЛАНАР —— НИКИТА ТОКАРЕВ
24 МАЯ В 17:00
4 МОСКОВСКАЯ БИЕННАЛЕ АРХИТЕКТУРЫ, ЦДХ,
ЭКСПОЗИЦИЯ АРХИТЕКТУРНОЙ ШКОЛЫ МАРШ, ЗАЛ 27

ДИСКУССИЯ #5
АРХИТЕКТУРНОЕ БЮРО ДЁШИНОВА И ГОЛЬДЕНБЕРГ —— КИРИЛЛ АСС
24 МАЯ В 17:00
4 МОСКОВСКАЯ БИЕННАЛЕ АРХИТЕКТУРЫ, ЦДХ,
ЭКСПОЗИЦИЯ АРХИТЕКТУРНОЙ ШКОЛЫ МАРШ, ЗАЛ 27

ДИСКУССИЯ #7
БЮРО FORM —— ВЛАДИМИР ПЛОТКИН
25 МАЯ В 16:00
4 МОСКОВСКАЯ БИЕННАЛЕ АРХИТЕКТУРЫ, ЦДХ,
ЭКСПОЗИЦИЯ АРХИТЕКТУРНОЙ ШКОЛЫ МАРШ, ЗАЛ 27

ДИСКУССИЯ #14
LE ATELIER —— АНАТОЛИЙ БЕЛОВ
30 МАЯ В 15:00
ЦДХ, 3 ЭТАЖ, ЗАЛ 17

ДИСКУССИЯ #15
NOWADAYS OFFICE —— АЛЕКСАНДР ОСТРОГОРСКИЙ
30 МАЯ В 15:00
ЦДХ, 3 ЭТАЖ, ЗАЛ 17

# Twopots Posters

This is a series of self-promotional posters of the studio, banking on powerful simplicity that defines their design concept. Fonts, space balancing and combination are what they are enthusiastic about.

**Studio: Twopots Design**
**Designer: Xavier Esclusa Trias**

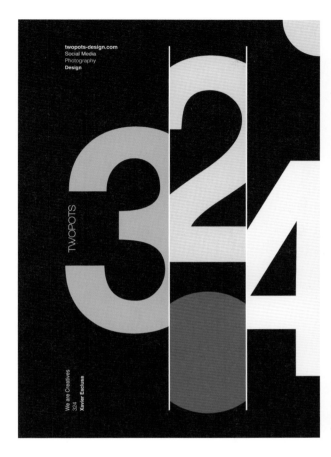

twopots-design.com
Social Media
Photography
**Design**

TWOPOTS

We are Creatives
324
Xavier Esclusa

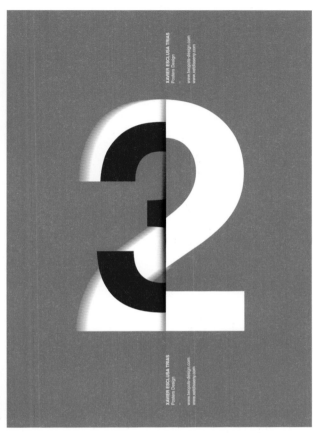

XAVIER ESCLUSA TRIAS
Posters Design
www.twopots-design.com
www.xetdisseny.com

XAVIER ESCLUSA TRIAS
Posters Design
www.twopots-design.com
www.xetdisseny.com

Branding / Website / Design     Stay hungry stay foolish     Twopots
www.xetdisseny.com
twopots-design.com

Xavier Esclusa Trias

Graphic Design Studio

www.twopots-design.com

www.xetdisseny.com

# Secrets of the Five Pictures

The book *Secrets of the Five Pictures* is a series of inspiring stories told by the film director Li Ding. The way that the designer constructed the five Arabic numerals from geometric shapes has challenged the graphic possibility of numerals and what a book cover should look like.

**Designer: Wang Zhi-Hong**

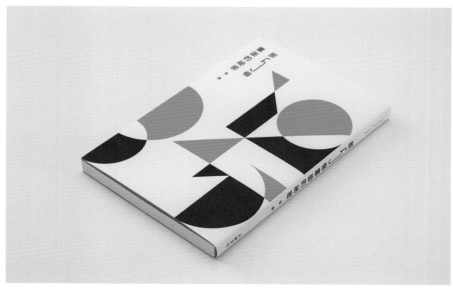

# Research Integrity

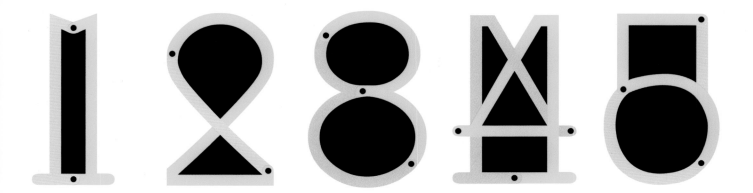

These books were designed for an academic seminar with the topic "Research Integrity". The designer made a gentle and elegant link between positive and negative numbers, aiming to express the idea that people exchange and communicate different views cordially.

**Designer: Cheng-Tsung Feng**

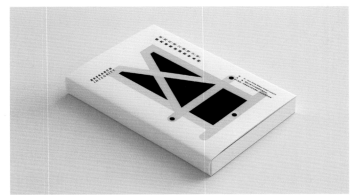

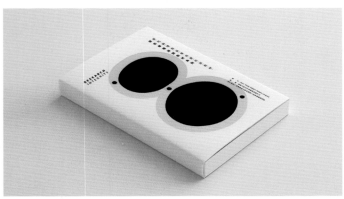

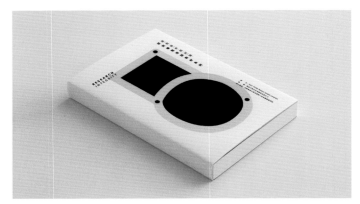